MW00628369

YOUR SECRET INHERITANCE

UNLOCKING YOUR TRUE POTENTIAL & REBOOTING YOUR LIFE

ROD WALZ

Copyright © 2020 Rod Walz All rights reserved

The characters and events portrayed in this book are fictitious. Any similarity to real persons, living or dead, is coincidental and not intended by the author.

No part of this book may be reproduced, or stored in a retrieval system, or transmitted in any form or by any means, electronic, mechanical, photocopying, recording, or otherwise, without express written permission of the publisher.

ISBN-13: 978-1-7350345-1-5

Printed in the United States of America

For more information and valuable tools visit:
http://www.yoursecretinheritance.com

CONTENTS

ACKNOWLEDGMENTS

I would not be the person and success I am today without the boost from some significant people in my life. First there was my mother who was a dear friend in my youth. always ready to listen. To a caring college professor, Ray McGowen, who coached me towards doubling up my Marketing major adding on an Education degree which set me on the path to be a high school teacher in NYC. To Renna Greenbaum, a teaching co-worker, I owe my first epiphany that reboot my life's direction in my early twenties. To Frank Lee, my manager at Victor Calculator Company for helping me to see how to use my informal talents in business. To John Haller, my patent attorney, who counseled me on a vision for branding my business using the WALZ name. To my wife Jeri for your wisdom and love who saw in me the incredible business potential I had at a time when

I was mired in limiting thought about what was possible. To PSI Seminars for their incredible courses designed to unleash the best in me by my looking inward and choosing a more fulfilled life. And finally, to my children who take life on like it is a vibrant laboratory for personal growth.

PRAISE FOR YOUR SECRET INHERITANCE

"Rod's unflinching honesty with the reader demonstrates how important it is to be honest with ourselves if we are to unlock our true potential. After hearing his journey, you will want to begin your own." – **Mark Fallon, CEO, The Berkshire Company**

"Rod Walz is a leader and role model for anyone who has a desire to grow. In this book, Rod helps us to understand how we have all developed limited thinking and beliefs that have had a powerful effect on our lives. More importantly, using his own life's experiences, he guides us through a pathway of discovery of our true limitless possibilities.

If you are seeking to achieve more in your life, this is a must read." – **Shirley Hunt, President, PSI Seminars**

ONE
A CHILD'S STORY

Let me tell you a story. It's a simple and short story about a young boy and his mother. When I say simple, I mean the action he took that day was simple in conventional terms, but the results were great and can be described as life altering. Here goes:

"A cup of tea would make her happy," the little boy, only six years old, thought as he put down his toys and rushed to the kitchen. He stopped and stared at the tall cabinets towering over him. He'd never made tea before but had watched his older siblings do it. Filled with determination and a burning desire, he set to the task of giving his mother the one thing she enjoyed immensely, hot tea.

The boy's mother had been restricted to her second-story bedroom due to severe rheumatoid arthritis, which left her debilitated and bedridden. The year was 1953, and at that time cortisone shots were the prescribed course of treatment, given daily. What wasn't known then was the treatment worsened the long-term effects of the disease, exacerbating her condition.

The boy grabbed the pot and, with the help of a stool, propped himself in front of the sink. As the water slowly filled the pot, his mind wandered to how happy his mother would be when he appeared in the doorway holding a cup of tea. Seeing this vision filled him with a greater joy and drove him to do everything perfectly.

From the sink to the stove he went, each movement deliberate and careful. Using both hands to lift the heavy pot, he set it on the burner and fiddled with the dial until a blue flame erupted. His eyes watched with amazement as the flames danced and licked the blackened bottom of the pot.

Onward he continued, this time to get a cup and saucer. He climbed up, opened the cabinet door and pulled out the cup. They were shallow and thin with a delicate handle on the side. He admired the cup as he held it gingerly in his small hands. He grabbed a saucer and got down as carefully as he had climbed up.

The last thing he needed was the tea bag itself. He knew right where they were. He opened a canister, and the aroma of dried tea leaves wafted over him. He pulled a single bag out and placed it into the cup.

He looked at everything he'd accomplished and was

filled with pride and anticipation. He glanced to the pot and saw the steam coming out. He turned the gas off and, recalling that it would be hot to the touch, used a potholder to pick it up. Using both hands and all his strength, he hovered the pot over the cup and poured. The hot water splashed into the cup, some of it spattering out, hitting the counter. A sweet subtle vapor rose from the steeping tea and covered his face.

With the cup full, he picked up the precious cargo with both hands and lowered himself off the stool. Anxious to get his gift to his mother, he marched through the dining room. When he reached the base of the stairs, he stopped. The more delicate maneuvering lay ahead of him, as he had to scale the seventeen steps to the landing above, then move down the long carpeted hallway to his mother's room. He took a deep breath and began his ascent, one careful step at a time until he crested the stairs. Happy to have completed that task, he stared down the dimly lit hall to his left.

The march to his mother's bedroom seemed far for a six-year-old, especially when he was carrying a hot cup of tea. Like he had done with the stairs, he put one carefully placed foot in front of the other. His eyes darted from watching the tea swish in the cup to the floor in front of him. His thoughts began to anticipate her response, and questions filled his mind: "Would she be happy? Would she be proud of him?"

As he passed the bathroom, on his right, he could finally see her through the open door of her room. Her frail body lay stretched out in the bed. He was so nervous when he reached the doorway but pushed aside his anxiety and entered the room. Careful to avoid the ever-present bedpan on the floor, he maneuvered himself to her bedside, stopped and quietly whispered, "Mommy, I've made you some tea."

She looked at him, sat up and peered at the cup in his hands. Her eyes widened and a big smile stretched across her face. "Honey, thank you so much," she said sweetly. She took the cup and continued to grin from ear to ear.

The boy watched with nervous eyes as she guided the cup to her lips and sipped.

"It tastes wonderful. Thank you so much for doing this. You've made me so happy," she said, her expression glowing with prideful delight at what he had done.

The boy's heart leapt with joy as he felt very special in her presence. He had wanted to make her happy, and he had, and in return he had also found happiness.

That boy would grow into a man, and years later he'd look back and realize that experience with his mother had been the foundational cornerstone of creating "WOW" moments in his life, both personal, through the deep connections he'd make with family and friends, and in business, with the products and services he'd bring to the world. Humorously, he'd sometimes imagine how different his life would have been if his mother had made nothing of the tea and didn't make him feel so appreciated. Would he have felt secure in taking risks and going for it in his life? Who knows!

The reason I know this story so intimately is because that boy is me. My name is Rod Walz, and throughout my career, I have often been asked, *when did I become an entrepreneur?* The answer became crystal clear in 2003, when I participated in the **PSI Seminar series (psiseminars.com)**, focusing on discovering how our early life's input forms the beliefs that affect how we show up in the present. It was during one of the seminars, I vividly recalled the experience I had at six years old above and how it created my first WOW experience, which led to everything I have created today. I now had my answer.

Thank you,

Mom.

TWO
WHAT IS YOUR SECRET INHERITANCE?

All of us have a secret inheritance inside our SubConscious Mind. This inheritance is so abundant and powerful that it stays with us the entire course of our life. It is persistent and will attract that which is familiar and will resist that which is new and different. Starting while in the womb, it expands rapidly after your birth and through your childhood. It becomes the operating system on which many of your current beliefs and actions are founded. The big question anyone reading might ask is "How do I know a secret inheritance exists?" Ask yourself this: "When did I choose to speak English (or your first language)?" Make sure you ask and answer this question before reading on. The obvious answer is you didn't choose, it was poured in *along with everything else*. (More about this in Chapter 4.)

Your Secret Inheritance is within you, and this book, in simple easy-to-follow terms, lays the groundwork to help you expose limiting thoughts created in your childhood, and learn approaches to create new thoughts that reset your life. You will discover how the Mind is typically on autopilot and that what we think is our authentic self may be nothing more than a rehash of old patterns. My life experiences, shared in this book, validate that your willingness to grow and be a great explorer of "self" is so worth it for a fulfilled life, with you in control.

The fundamental principle we will focus on is that as a child you had all kinds of other people's beliefs poured into your *unfiltered* SubConscious Mind, when you had no vote or veto. This very fact significantly affects your behavior and attitudes today. You were an active participant, as a young child, reacting to those beliefs and making decisions about yourself. For example, if what got poured into you was that you are an incredible child and loved, you may decide that this is true and set a path forward believing that. On the other hand, if you had, for example, an abusive parent who told you that you were no good, you may decide that you weren't that good and not worthy of happiness. If all this is true, you can see how important it is to understand what got poured into your soil, which molded the "you" you are today.

My spiritual work focuses on creating an evolving vision for my life, continuing to uncover my limiting beliefs, and sharing what I have learned with others. To empower your life, it is very helpful to understand what you have been dragging around in your hidden self-beliefs. Use what you read about here to reactivate that joyful, inquisitive child within while I take you on a journey through my life, as well as others' lives. My life is a vivid demonstration of the empowerment and growth that you can experience when overcoming inherited limiting beliefs. You will see that much of my work, shared in this book, is focused on my relationship with money because this was the area in my life where I was most stuck. I assure you that what we will talk about applies in every aspect of your life.

Like you, I had other people's beliefs poured into me and I made decisions about myself and my capabilities based on those early beliefs. Many of those beliefs moved me forward, and many of those beliefs held me back. The dilemma for me was that one of the beliefs poured into me was that it was not right for me to challenge these beliefs. Once I woke up and understood my right to challenge them, "my authentic life" took flight in a way I never imagined. It is no fluke that this average kid from Brooklyn grew into a highly successful entrepreneur while simultaneously creating a powerful and loving marriage with my wife, Jeri, and our children, for the past forty years.

These are a few of the highlights:

- Early seventies, created breakthrough programs and approaches that changed the lives of inner-city students as the Dean of Boys at Thomas Jefferson High School in Brooklyn, NY.
- 1975, created the first automated system for use in determining Financial Aid grants for college students, used nationwide.
- 1982, introduced the Electra Foreclosure System, the first automated system designed to create and print all the documents for processing foreclosures in California, replacing the labor-intensive and mistake-prone typewriters that had been used until then.
- 1983, created the multi-patented Walz Certified Mailer© and software, which revolutionized how large users of Certified Mail handled critical communications. Walz Certified Mailers have been used in approximately 300,000,000 transactions, saving millions of labor hours for our clients.
- 1990, created the Walz Item Tracking System

(WITS), the first system to replace the laborious manual logging systems for organizations that receive large volumes of accountable items, such as packages from FedEx, UPS, US Postal Service (USPS), internal critical documents, etc.

- 2001, started Walz Secured Outsourcing services, which focuses on compliant centric processing and mailing of delinquency notices for the mortgage industry, ultimately providing these critical services for up to 50% of all delinquency notices mailed in the United States.

- 2015, after thirty-three years, brought about the sale of the WALZ Group, giving Jeri and me the freedom to live our dreams and contribute wherever we desire.

———

WHY I WROTE THIS BOOK

The above didn't happen by chance or luck. What I've been able to accomplish is a direct result of challenging those limited beliefs, then taking immediate action on my vision. This takes me to why I wrote this book. I feel blessed in becoming aware of how over-coming limiting beliefs leads to growth in all areas of my life, and I am so excited to share what I have discovered. I especially want to reach you if you have a burning desire and willingness to grow and want a bigger, bolder and happier life. Even if you are not there yet, I wrote this for you if you want more and want to better your circumstances. Sometimes you may feel shackled or stuck and notice you are just cruising by. Yet you still sense that life can offer something greater than what you are currently experiencing. It can and will if you do the internal work as an explorer of self.

 "...change your mantra from *this is who I am* to *this is who I am becoming*"

Let me be clear that I bless everyone's right to choose how they live their life. However, it does make me sad when I hear someone complain about their life as though they have no power over it. This could not be further from the truth. Each and every one of us is *responsible and accountable* for our lives and has all the *power* to alter it. If you are willing to change your mantra from *this is who I am* to *this is who I am becoming*, life's ample abundance is available and ready to respond. You'll notice that in answering why I wrote this book, I didn't mention "money". The lessons in this book relate to everything in our life experience; however, I chose, in the book, to focus on my financial consciousness because money is so clear and measurable. For example, when I was making $20,000 per year, that was a measure of my financial consciousness and that is perfectly ok. If you think of money as an exchange of value, it begins to make more sense. Years ago, we traded goats and pigs as the value exchange. Now we use dollars. My life was never focused on chasing money. As I later learned, for me if I did that, money would just keep moving away because of my internal value system. Conversely, my life's journey is about overcoming my limited beliefs in every aspect of my life and especially in the area of money. I never kept track of the money I made because I stayed focused on creating more value. Thanks to my wife, Jeri, the money is tracked.

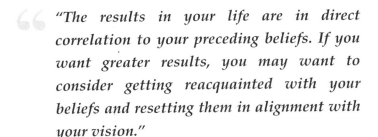

> *"The results in your life are in direct correlation to your preceding beliefs. If you want greater results, you may want to consider getting reacquainted with your beliefs and resetting them in alignment with your vision."*

TAMMY'S STORY

———

This story is an excellent example of someone who was willing to take responsibility for her life and get vulnerable (not so safe). The result was immediate.

As part of my journey, I have been a speaker at some industry-focused conventions. Usually my topics surround specific industry-related concepts. However, at this one particular convention, they said I could speak on any topic I wanted, so I did. The theme of the talk was "US AND THEM". It focused on how we are raised in an *us and them* culture from our birth. The ultimate message of my talk was that all of us are connected, and all of us are personally accountable in our life.

After my talk, a woman (I'll call her Tammy) approached me and shared how moved she was about the things I'd pointed out, especially about how we are completely responsible for the results in our life. She wanted my advice on how to deal with a work situation with her boss. I asked her if she dwells on how others view her, and she emphatically answered yes, which brought us back to her issue with her boss. I asked her, "What's the issue?" Tammy pointed out how embarrassed she was about her weight and that, because of it, she thought others didn't really see how great she was, including her boss, who had not given her a raise in some time. She had a built-in story that her boss had some bias and her weight was a contributing factor. I coached her to take full responsibility (not blame her boss) and meet with him and ask, "What is it about me that gets in the way of getting a raise?" She promised me she would do it.

About a week later Tammy called me with the news that she had received not only a raise but a promotion. I asked her what had happened, and she told me how she went into the meeting with her boss with a shifted attitude that he was a professional and a good man. Tammy addressed the issue of her not having a raise and asked him, "What is it about me that gets in the way of getting a raise?" He gave her important feedback on some of her work habits, which were not productive, along with some other issues. He was especially impressed with the way in which she approached him so responsibly. This further opened up the discussion about what was next for her. It was then he suggested not only a raise but also a promotion. She cried in gratitude and self-reflection on the phone. I let her know that all I did was hold up a mirror and she did the work.

What Tammy had done was shift her belief away from victim consciousness and become open to the belief that she was completely responsible and accountable for her own life. That small shift resulted in immediate results. It's a powerful and real account to illustrate how detrimental limited beliefs can be and how quickly our lives can change once we align our beliefs with our vision. Ponder this going forward. *"The results in your life are in direct correlation to your preceding beliefs. If you want greater results, you may want to consider getting reacquainted with your beliefs and resetting them in alignment with your vision."* Hopefully, as you read the book, this statement will evolve in your understanding and appreciation.

———

THE PATH AHEAD

Maybe you want a clear blueprint on how you can break through and be more of your authentic self. What I offer is a path, but it is up to you to do the work and walk that path. In that direction, you'll be covering the following topics:

- **Overcoming Limited Beliefs**
- **Money Consciousness**
- **Aligning Your Beliefs with your Vision**
- **Surround Yourself with Those Who Will Support Your Vision**
- **Why Am I In the Presence Of**
- **Everything Happens Within You**
- **Tools, Stories and Insights from My Journey**

On each topic I'll dive in deeper and fully explain and also illustrate using my own life and experiences as an example to give texture so that it will be easier for you to understand and apply them to your own life.

As you turn the pages ahead, you'll be taken on a journey that's the story of my life. You'll go from my days in Brooklyn, New York, where I had my first epiphany, to California, where my life professionally blossomed and where I met the love of my life, Jeri. It is here where my second epiphany took place. Each story will give you a fuller picture of how I overcame limited beliefs, tapped into my authentic self, and turned an ordinary life into an extraordinary one. Each and every one of you also has that authentic self who sits inside you, waiting to come out.

I am so honored that you're here and feel blessed that I have this opportunity to share the tools and lessons from my life. I am also grateful to the many people I have met who were willing to grow and choose to take growth on as a full-time mission. You have inspired me along the way.

Because it has to be said, some of what you'll read will probably clash with long-held and deep-seated beliefs of your own. I ask that you set those aside as you read. Be open and willing to experience something new, yet familiar. What's the worst that can happen? You can always go back to how you viewed life before.

Before we head into the next chapter, I'll leave you with a quote from one of my favorite authors, Richard Bach. I find him so poignant and reflective, enjoy.

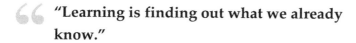 **"Learning is finding out what we already know."**

THREE

THE BASICS OF THE MIND

To get us started, it would help to discuss some fundamentals of how the mind works so you can have a clearer understanding of where I am taking you on this journey. The following is a simple, common-sense explanation of what is going on in that mind of yours.

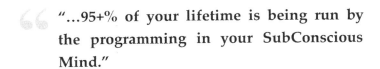

"...95+% of your lifetime is being run by the programming in your SubConscious Mind."

The mind is made up of three parts:

- Conscious Mind
- SubConscious Mind
- SuperConscious Mind

Conscious Mind

The best way to explain this is to invite you to become aware of this present moment as you read these words. Become aware of holding this book (or device if you're reading the e-book), notice your breathing, feel the position of your body, feel the bottoms of your feet, notice the temperature in the room and the sounds around you. This is your Conscious Mind, plain and simple. Basically, it is in your Conscious Mind where we *observe* (as I just asked you to do) and *choose* what's next. In essence, if you ever wanted to answer the esoteric question of *who am I*, it might be found in the simplistic view that you are simply an Observer and a Chooser, most of the rest comes from your SubConscious beliefs about yourself, positive and negative, that got poured into you by life when you were a child, with no vote and no veto.

 "Most child development experts agree that in the first five years of development, 50% of our personality is formed, and that number grows to 85% by eight years old."

SubConscious Mind

This data repository contains all your individual and

collective memories, as well as your reactions and behaviors as a result of those memories. It is where your beliefs reside. Different than most repositories, it actively combines thoughts and experiential memories, which collectively become your traits, your habits and your personality. It also uses all the data and makes very strong suggestions as to how you should believe, think and act. In essence, it is a repository of all the things your Conscious Mind experiences, including mental and emotional imprints from your past. It then shows up as programming, almost akin to an operating system that is going twenty-four seven, running your bodily functions as well as the majority of life's moments. This all happens whether or not you are even aware it is doing so. **Consider that 95+% of your lifetime is being run by the programming in your SubConscious Mind.** How much of that programming came to you voluntarily? How much was poured into you? How much of what is in your SubConscious Mind is authentically yours? These are good questions to ask.

Most importantly, be very aware of your conscious thoughts because those thoughts will drive the direction of your life going forward as they embed themselves onto your SubConscious Mind. This puts new meaning to the phrase "Watch your language". However, in this context, it means watching how you talk to yourself, because how you communicate with yourself can have a lasting effect because it embeds itself into your SubConscious Mind, then shows up later in either a positive or negative way. I have found playing golf to be a great way to find out how you speak to yourself. Let's say I just hit a ball out of bounds. Do I calmly say, "Well, that was interesting," or do I say, "You stupid idiot, Rod." I can assure you that the latter used to come out of me more often than I care to admit. Now I use golf as a growth experience, and I have chosen to be kinder to myself and spend a moment thinking about what in my swing caused the ball to go out of bounds. Well, mostly. (LOL)

The SubConscious Mind can support your vision for where you want to go, while at the same time, if you're not paying attention, can be a strong and vocal advocate for limiting your vision.

While there are certain moments where we are consciously present, more often than not, we operate on automatic pilot. We eat the same food over and over, listen to our "favorite" music, drive our cars while focused on other thoughts, etc., all based upon the thoughts directed from our SubConscious Mind. It's amazing how it knows how to drive our car while we engage on a cell phone call discussing business. Have you ever asked yourself who drove the car the last couple of miles? My wife, Jeri, reminds me I don't do this very well.

Other than your DNA and chromosomal engineering, at birth, our SubConscious Mind is a "tabula rasa", which, in Latin, means "blank slate". When we start out as a baby, life experiences get poured into us. This is an extremely important concept to grasp because most of us don't realize the "who I am" that we think we are is founded on the thoughts, beliefs and experiences of others who poured them into us at a time when we had no vote or veto. By the way, this is not good or bad, it's just what is. **Most child development experts agree that in the first five years of development, 50% of our personality is formed, and that number grows to 85% by eight years old.**

Unbeknownst to us consciously, we made *early subtle decisions* about our worthiness/unworthiness, our feeling of being heard/not heard, our feelings of being loved/the ability to love, our willingness or lack thereof to step up and take the lead, our willingness to question/challenge concepts and beliefs, our capabilities and our fears, etc.

Our very early influencers, the people or things that shaped our personality and core beliefs, were our mother, father, alternate parents, brothers, sisters, religion, teachers, good friends, bad friends, physical and emotional hurts, positive wins, losses, etc., and this all happened in our formative years.

An interesting thought to consider is how old your

mom was when you were born, and what open and limited thoughts permeated her thinking that were passed on by *her* early life influencers, then were poured into you. What's important to comprehend is that these foundational memories, thoughts and experiences permeate how we show up as adults.

> "The SubConscious Mind will faithfully coordinate your decision-making thoughts and feelings along three themes: keep everything *familiar*, keep me *safe*, and keep me *right* (not wrong)."

Conscious Mind's relationship with the SubConscious Mind: Every conscious thought has the ability to affect the beliefs carried by the SubConscious Mind. However, the SubConscious Mind is conditioned to sort what it hears and experiences into old familiar tracks. The encouraging news is that new conscious thoughts, which are repeatedly sent to the SubConscious Mind, will eventually evolve the old thoughts into new patterns or beliefs. The term "you can't teach an old dog new tricks" isn't true.

To give the new thoughts some juice, it is the emotional connection to this new thought that is the amperage needed to change your inner beliefs and patterns. This is important. Just having intellectual thoughts won't cut it, you must *see it and feel it* too. Without an emotional connection to this new thought, the subconscious can tend to dwindle back to the old familiar infrastructure. Einstein put it best: "**You can't solve a problem with the same thinking that got you into it.**" Meaning you can't get clear at the subconscious level by staying in your logical and scientific conscious head. This path to changing one's consciousness takes ongoing discipline with a commitment to growth and change.

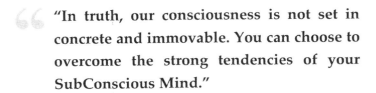

"**In truth, our consciousness is not set in concrete and immovable. You can choose to overcome the strong tendencies of your SubConscious Mind.**"

The SubConscious Mind will faithfully coordinate your decision-making thoughts and feelings along three themes: keep everything *familiar*, keep me *safe*, and keep me *right* (not wrong). In essence, it has a job to do. Let's explore this:

Familiar:

This is probably the strongest element of the Subconscious Mind because it has been given the job of keeping everything familiar and the same. Because it is so powerful, we will share a few examples.

Think about areas in your life where this is true. For

example, you grew up in one religion and you meet someone of another faith, and you want to deepen the relationship. Your parents and early influencers, in all likelihood, had poured in a belief that you should stay within your faith. Without anyone knowing about the relationship, you begin to question yourself if the relationship could work in the long term. What's tough to figure out is whether your questioning is "authentic" or is it just the Subconscious Mind doing its job and fighting to keep you the same. To make the point further, there was a commercial from the '70s for Memorex, a major manufacturer of audiocassette tapes, whereby Ella Fitzgerald would sing a high note and a wineglass would shatter. The punch line from the commercial was **"Is it live or is it Memorex?"** In this case the punch line regarding your questioning is **"Is it you or is it your Subconscious Mind?"** Well worth exploring.

Another great example of "familiar" happened in my life. In my family, I was the youngest of six siblings. We went onto the following vocations: housewife, perennial student, college professor, nurse, teacher and then me, teacher. See a familiar pattern here. Nowhere was anybody inclined towards money as the key motivator. Absolutely nothing wrong with that, and these choices were quite noble and very "familiar" with the way I grew up. For me to break out of this familiar pattern and become the financial success I became, I had to completely change my thinking (my mental DNA).

Probably one of the biggest examples of the SubConscious Mind at work is in the expression **"this is just how I am"** as though you are stuck in concrete consciousness. I know that I have said these exact words, especially when someone dear to me is challenging me to grow and I'm not in the mood. I have also seen it in others when someone challenges them to grow or take a different perspective and they respond, "This is just how I am." Take a look into your life and recall if you have ever responded with "This is just how I am" when someone has pushed you to grow or take a different perspective. Try on **"Who am I becoming?"** and see how different you feel in your soul. We will cover this in more detail later on.

Another example of the power of the SubConscious Mind worth noting revolves around children of alcoholic parents. I have met men and women who grew up in homes with alcoholic parents who vow they will never be like them. Yet they find themselves in a destructive alcoholic marriage and don't grasp that they are here because it is "familiar" territory. A theme you will hear multiple times in this book is **we attract to ourselves life experiences at the level of our consciousness.** The SubConscious Mind is doing the attracting, and your Conscious Mind might just have a blind spot.

In truth, our consciousness is not set in concrete and immovable. You can choose to overcome the strong tendencies of your SubConscious Mind.

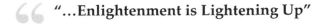 **"...Enlightenment is Lightening Up"**

I will leave you with one final example, from my life, that demonstrates the above. I mentioned PSI Seminars in Chapter One. In 2003, I was taking a PSI Men's Leadership experiential course with over 100 men. It took place on PSI's ranch in northern California. We all lived on campus in open dorms with bunk beds (never heard so much snoring in my life). The weeklong seminar consisted of numerous experiential exercises designed to help you look within. During one of the exercises, we (men) walked around this big open room, in silence, as the facilitator would make suggestions for things to focus on. The last point he made was to notice how you only make eye contact with certain men and others you dismiss for no apparent reason and don't make eye contact. When the exercise was over, the facilitator instructed us to remain in silence throughout the night and following morning, when we would rejoin for breakfast. He also suggested we consider taking a meditative walk, alone, the next morning before breakfast, thinking about this evening's exercise and what we may have discovered about ourselves.

Well, I opted to go on that walk, and then he appeared. It was an Italian guy from Las Vegas on my path (I grew up relating to my mother's Irish side, and most of my neighbors were Irish). I noticed that I wanted to avoid him because I was full of judgment. Even though I had never had a conversation with him, I had observed him speaking and decided he must be arrogant and not like me (ha ha). When I heard my thoughts and reflected on the exercise from the following night, I decided to break through my bias and go up and meet him. I got within thirty feet of him, turned left and took what I called my "chicken exit".

I found myself alone and plopped myself down and started crying. While crying, I started my internal conversation, first saying how I do this all the time, chicken out when facing this particular bias, judgment of certain men. I then asked my inner child, Gerard (Gerard is my birth name), to help me. Immediately, I was transported in my mind to my mother's bedroom at six years old. I had just come into her room after being out playing with two new boys I had never met before (we had a lot of freedom back then). Being bedridden, my mommy sat up and asked me to share about the wonderful time I had with them. This went on for a bit, and then it happened. She asked me if they were Catholic, and I answered no. We spoke no further and I left the room.

I never played with those boys again because, at six years old, I already had a belief that I thought was real because it was inside me. In essence, I was cooked!

Now for the great stuff. Here I was, plopped down on the ground with a realization that my prejudice was not mine, but rather it had been given to me by my mommy and others. I had already had it in 1953 at six years old, and I saw clearly that I had inherited someone else's belief. Now I felt awakened and went back in meditation to speak with my mother (she died in 1966). I sat on her bed as little Gerard and spoke to her, as I would back then, and basically said, "Mommy, I'm much older now and have learned much in my fifty-six years on earth. I found out that we are all connected and that each of us is special in the eyes of God. I know that you are always doing what you think is best and that much of what you believe came from your father and mother. I hope you will learn from this, and I want you to know that even though this belief (being Catholic is the only way) became a metaphor for other biases I had, I forgive you and love you for who you truly are." I felt such a release from this bias.

I was ecstatic and went and found "the Italian" and shared how much he had meant to me. We hugged and cried together, and he said he was glad his presence helped me break through.

Since that day, I have completely allowed myself to be open to friendships with other men. When I traveled a lot through airports, I would purposely seat myself next to a man in the waiting area and start up a conversation. What I found out was that these men were really boys in men's skin bags with a rich and full life's story.

After these "familiar" examples showing how the SubConscious Mind loves to keep you under control, I thought I'd share some lighthearted *("enlightenment is lightening up")* things to break some of your SubConscious Mind's automatic and familiar patterns. The following are some simple techniques that I have had fun with (**make up your own and try it on**):

- Reverse the direction of your toilet paper roll.
- Brush your teeth with the opposite hand.
- Eat with the fork in your opposite hand.
- Order something unique to you on the menu.
- Find something good in someone you don't like.
- Tell someone you normally wouldn't tell that you love and respect them (if you do).

Safe:

Imagine being in New York City and you step off the curb and a taxi is heading towards you at 40 mph. This is absolutely not the time for your Conscious Mind to be involved. It is your SubConscious Mind that assesses the danger, takes over and pulls you back onto the sidewalk. As dramatic as this seems, the SubConscious Mind does this in all aspects of your emotional experience, as well. For example, how many of us find ourselves in a relationship, either personally or professionally, where we spend an inordinate amount of time playing it safe? We hide out, don't communicate, and hope for the best. It seems like the right thing to do, but it exacerbates the inevitable. We need to step up and express what is true for us. Get vulnerable, get unsafe.

During my journey, I have spoken with numerous entrepreneurs who told me how, when they shared their idea to take a risk, it was often their own families and friends who suppressed them the most. In their own minds, the families and friends often didn't realize they were letting their own fear (their Subconscious Mind about keeping things Safe) dominate their input. Many times, they didn't ask about why this new venture **will be** successful. Instead, they focused on cautioning them about the downsides without exploring the upsides. Obviously, they cared; however, it is a valid question to ask what drove their input and cautions.

FYI, what I like about the earlier story I shared about Tammy is that she chose to get vulnerable and walked through her fear of rejection and overcame playing it safe.

Right:

Sorry to tell you this, being "right" is the booby prize. The SubConscious Mind has been conditioned to maintain a state of consciousness where you always end up on the **"right" side of the equation**. Of course, it is important to keep the facts straight in any situation. As it pertains to a relationship (family, friend, spouse, co-worker, etc.) if one person isn't playing fair or is off-kilter, certainly it is important to keep tabs on the issues. However, the habit and **need to be right** can also be a great inhibitor to a healthy relationship.

The problem with being "right" is that you feel so justified, logical and factual, and you could be missing some incredible potential for growth.

Using a marriage example (applies to all relationships, friends, co-workers, boss, etc.), your SubConscious Mind has a tendency to build up a "being-right case" against your partner, starting with petty offenses. At first, you don't see the blind spot, as it seems harmless and normal being right because of the familiarity of the relationship over time. However, if unchecked with honest communication, you run the risk of creating a deepening divide in the marriage and potential for failure. The earlier you can recognize that "your need to be right" is what really is behind your thoughts, the better. You then can have an honest communication with your partner about your thoughts and, combined with a good listening ear on your part, it can make for a phenomenal relationship instead of the alternative.

If you are interested in exploring this further, Tony Robbins developed a master class on this in his **Ultimate Relationship Seminar** (available on DVD), where he takes a couple from the oblivion of "being right" and helps them get beyond that and discover they have the ability to provide for each other's basic needs for *Certainty, Uncertainty, Significance* and *Love and Connection*.

As I said, it is truly a master class, and I recommend it for everyone. Jeri and I completely reinvigorated our relationship through his course at a time when we were feeling very disconnected after twenty-nine years of marriage and questioned our future together. I felt so **"right"** and so did Jeri. Once we truly "listened to each other" (without reacting) about what "needs" were not being met, the forgiveness and empathy for each other took over and the deep feeling of love reappeared. For the record, once we realized we simply were not meeting each other's needs, our SubConscious Minds shut down being right and the rest was relatively easy because we now had a simple formula to relate to. Since that moment, Jeri and I fell deeper and deeper in love. I honestly can tell you that, after forty years of marriage, I love her more today than ever. One of the great questions I ask each day is "what does Jeri need from me today?" Pure magic in a relationship.

Remember, when dealing with others, notice if you are coming from a position of being right versus truly listening to the other person's point of view. You might be surprised what you create when you lay down your righteousness sword.

"What if every thought is a prayer?"

————

SuperConscious Mind

This is the area of the mind where connection to the infinite occurs (God, Universe, Universal Mind, Infinite Intelligence, whatever you relate to). Have you ever found yourself inspired by a new thought or dream you never had before? Where did that come from? Your SubConscious Mind is very limited in scope because it relies on past experience to operate. Your SuperConscious Mind is unlimited and available to all there is in the universe. You can call on it anytime you want. Tapping into this power is something most of the global influencers, over time, knew very well. They realized that thoughts and intuition came through you and not from you.

Paramhansa Yogananda was an Indian yogi and guru who introduced millions of Indians and Westerners to the teachings of meditation. He said that, "Thoughts are universally, not individually, rooted." In other words, the SuperConscious Mind is the pathway of communication with God/Universe. *What if every thought is a prayer?* If true, it is so important to **think about what we are thinking about** *all the time*. I was raised in a belief that God answers all our prayers. So, if our thoughts/prayers come from a limited consciousness, such as "I'm not worthy of abundance", God/Universe may respond in kind. Conversely, if my thought is "I am worthy of abundance", God/Universe has more to work with in responding to that thought.

Many years ago, I embraced the thought that **we attract to ourselves at the level of our consciousness**. This means that "we are what we think about". For example, if you are open to the thought that you are connected through the SuperConscious Mind and have a clear vision of attracting money in your life, you become fertile ground for financial abundance to come your way. Conversely, if you stay in your SubConscious Mind and there is an embedded belief that "money is the root of all evil", and you accept that belief, in all likelihood you will not attract (create) money in your life.

Generally speaking, the Conscious Mind sees every-thing as separate from each other. A table is only a table, a person is simply the body they inhabit and nothing more. It has a very limited view of the world around it. Conversely, the SuperConscious Mind sees that every-thing is, in reality, made of energy and consciousness and, therefore, it sees the underlying unity behind the outer forms. In essence, **everything is connected**.

It is here, in the SuperConscious realm, where our vision for our life is amplified. All my successes reside here. Tapping into this power has been my greatest asset, for it is here where my new thoughts and ideas came from. Intuition and imagination have been the bridge between my Conscious and SuperConscious Mind. I encourage you to be a brave and relentless explorer in this realm, for it is here where the manifestation of your visionary thoughts are formed.

Now that you understand the three distinct parts of the mind, it will be easier to understand what I'm going to share later on. It will help you to better understand the source of your inherited limiting beliefs and illustrate your given power to alter them if you see that these limiting beliefs are not serving you. Speaking about altering your beliefs, I have included a very effective process at the end of the book that can retrain your mind to listen to you versus it being in control of your thoughts.

FOUR
OVERCOMING LIMITED BELIEFS

A s I mentioned in the previous chapter, your beliefs are imbedded in your SubConscious Mind of how you think about yourself, even today, and were poured into you as a child with no vote or veto. The only way to truly overcome any of those limited beliefs that are holding you back is to understand that nothing is fixed or permanent, and you can choose to change it.

————

When Did You Choose To Speak English?

"When did you choose to speak English" or whatever your first language is? You didn't choose, which begs another question: *what else got poured in*? This line of questioning is a wonderful place to start your journey to better understand how you operate in the world and what might be standing in the way of your greatness.

For me, there was a time when I was frustrated with my life and the results I had created. I desperately wanted to better understand what was limiting me. I'd look around and see other people doing better than I was; they weren't necessarily more intelligent than I was, didn't have a leg up, so to speak, yet they were making more money and had greater influence.

When I pondered on the reality that I had not *chosen* to speak English but rather it was poured into me by my parents and early influencers, I began questioning and challenging *every belief.* I began asking "what do **I** authentically believe about (fill in the blank)?"

———

THE GLASS

" "…the two most influencing components are *love and worthiness.*"

The best way to illustrate the above is by imagining you're holding an empty glass. The glass represents your life. Your hand is you, *the holder of your life*. Now take ice cubes, one by one, and put them in. Each cube represents each element that got poured into your life, making up the center of your core beliefs and personality.

The first cube represents your being given a human body imbedded with DNA and chromosomes that set a foundation for your life. The next cubes are your mother's open and closed mindset about everything; your father's open and closed mindset about everything (think about their age and maturity when you were born); early influencers (legal guardians, grandparents, teachers, etc.); your siblings' interaction with you; religion; moral and ethical beliefs; worthiness and unworthiness input; being loved and not being loved input; feeling safe and not feeling safe input; etc. All of these influencers are now embedded in your glass (life).

In my experience, the two most influencing components are *love and worthiness*. They are the centerpiece of your inherited consciousness and affect so deeply the results in your life regarding love, happiness and economic results. Imagine if you experienced, early on, that you were not loved and capable of giving love, how do you think your life will turn out relationship wise? Imagine if, early on, you had experiences of not feeling worthy (it could be about anything), how do you think you would turn out results wise? In my inner work and my work supporting others, I found these two elements (love and worthiness) at the centerpiece of life's successes and challenges.

So here you now stand, as the holder of your life, with a glass full of life elements you had no vote or veto over. In a perfect world, you would consider looking at each individual element to understand your makeup, your personality. However, something happened along the way. The ice cubes melted, and you are now the holder of a blend of elements that have come together as a theme called your personality and core beliefs. In reality, you may be a sum of other people's qualities (plus and minus) that you believe are yours, when in truth they aren't. Because these qualities (beliefs) are familiar, it is easy to ride the flow and never truly change to a more authentic self even when life gives you opportunities to do so. There is nothing wrong with maintaining the status quo, and in reality, most people's needle of change moves only a little bit. I can tell you with certainty that when you see someone you admire doing great things in their life, their needle has moved significantly beyond the beliefs that got poured in.

————

My First Epiphany/Transformation in Consciousness

"You do get to ask why in your life."

I grew up in an Irish Catholic neighborhood in Brooklyn, NY, in the 1950s, the youngest of six children (three boys and three girls). Brooklyn, at that time, was a very safe place. Our doors were unlocked, and we were free to roam as kids, out playing every conceivable game.

Our lives were from another world of consciousness compared to the current bent-over necks of whole populations of children (and adults) imbedded and addicted to "technology as play".

My dad had an incredible work ethic, working for the same company all his adult life in accounting and then as controller of the company. He was generally a quiet man, while on occasion the little boy would come out. As mentioned earlier, my mother had become stricken with severe arthritis earlier, and after my birth, it set in hard. The term "bedridden" became a normal and customary word describing her condition. I pretty much only knew her in bed most of my life until she died in 1966.

She and my father were deeply religious and indoctrinated in the Catholic dogma and experience. We all went to Catholic schools, most of us through college. The church was the centerpiece of our community, including for me, a great sports program called the CYO (Catholic

Youth Organization), where I thrived in baseball. My mother was an incredible woman and friend. She was raised in an era where her whole life centered on being at home and raising her kids. My dad was the breadwinner and very frugal.

Deeply imbedded in our upbringing was the belief that we as Catholics were the "one" true church. This very concept so limited our view of the world and molded a very limited consciousness about the diversity that existed in our local world.

My bedridden mother was a devoted Catholic, and we felt it. There would be no other point of view, period. I was an altar boy, went to Mass and Communion multiple times a week, and knew God was always watching. I believed I should spend my life doing everything necessary for salvation in heaven.

As I entered my teen years, the fear of salvation deepened as puberty set in. Need I say more? Even though I grew up as the youngest of six children, without anyone knowing, I felt so alone. At fourteen years old, I found a young girl to love and "take care of", a familiar inner theme given how I felt important caring for my bedridden mother. Everyone, including my parents, tried to get through to me. "You are too young to have a committed relationship with someone who is facing some tough issues of her own." Did I listen? No!

During those years from fourteen to twenty-one, I

tried to break off from my girlfriend, including when we were engaged. Each time the reaction was devastating to her, and each time I acted as hero, which was *familiar*, changing my mind and continuing the pattern of being a good boy and putting my needs second. Roll forward to 1968, I graduated from St. John's University in June, and a week later we were getting married at my local parish, St. Vincent Ferrer, with a Nuptial Mass and all. I placed myself at the front of the church while the organ played "Here Comes the Bride". What no one knew but me was that my internal dialogue with myself was *"Now, I will never have what I want in my life."* Basically, at twenty-one, I thought my "chosen" life was over.

We returned from our honeymoon and I set out to be a teacher in the NYC high school system. It wasn't until the week after school started that I got a call about an opening at Louis Brandeis High School, which served the upper west side of Manhattan and Harlem. The job was teaching Distributive Education (aka retailing) to mostly inner-city kids. So here I was, at twenty-one, walking into a class full of African American and Puerto Rican students.

I remember vividly the moment I walked into my first class. I soon broke out in laughter, and the kids asked me why I was laughing. I told them my background as a white, Catholic boy, who went to all white Catholic schools, and that I had never been in the presence of people of color until then. They seemed to like my honesty, so I continued. I asked them to make a deal with me. The deal was that they would teach me "how to be with them" in exchange for me doing my best to teach them the curriculum I had a responsibility to convey. I made that covenant with them by shaking the hand of each student to seal the deal. We both honored our original deal and had a great semester together.

In my department, there was a fellow teacher named Renna Greenbaum. She and I became friends in the friend's sense. I kept her posted on my life, and she was aware that my wife was pregnant; however, she was not aware of my inner, most private thoughts that I alone knew. One day, at lunch, she blurted out how excited she was for me that the baby was due in March, about four months away. Suddenly this wave of emotion swelled up and I burst out crying. She knew enough about me to know I was in trouble with my "self". She invited me to meet her after school and go for a walk.

As we walked down Broadway, in Manhattan, she encouraged me to open up and tell her what the tears were about. I proceeded to tell her about my life and that I realized you don't necessarily get the life you wanted. She said you get to choose your life, and you are allowed to question it as well. Overcome with emotion, I raised my voice and yelled at her, *"Renna, you don't get to ask why in your life. You have to accept your life the way it is.*" With that, this demure Jewish girl from the Bronx reached up, grabbed me by the lapel, shook me hard and hollered back, "You *do* get to ask why in your life."

To my surprise, I trusted Renna and, for the first time in my life, *gave myself permission to question everything about my life.*

As I rode home on the subway that afternoon, I was filled with excitement, knowing I gave myself permission to ask why. Then reality set in. How did I find a way to tell my wife, pregnant with our daughter, of my epiphany and excitement for my life going forward? I was not emotionally intelligent in this area and decided honesty was best and proceeded to share with her my innermost thoughts, past and present. Let's just say it didn't go well.

I took immediate action and sought counseling. Through those sessions, I realized I had to question everything I believed in, I mean everything. It was clear that I couldn't do this halfway because I intuitively knew if I did, the old patterns would creep right back. Expanding on my action, I eventually left my wife and went to live with my dad. As you can imagine, this was not an easy time for all involved, especially when my daughter, Kym, was born.

In the midst of everything that was happening at that time, I also found myself without employment in 1969, as my position at Brandies High School was eliminated.

Fortunately, later on that year I was hired at Thomas Jefferson High School in the East New York area Brooklyn. Jefferson was an inner-city school with a student population challenged by all the elements of inner-city life. For safety, we had two NYC police officers assigned on campus. In my first year there, I again felt the pinch of budget cuts, and my position was eliminated. However, I was well respected, so in my second year I was appointed as a permanent substitute teacher, filling in every day.

I loved the kids very much there and saw that the current Dean of Boys' hard-handed approach wasn't working, as the kids were struggling because of it. It was then that I volunteered in the Boys' Dean's office, which was responsible for student safety and discipline. I did have a hidden agenda, making myself invaluable. I spent every free period in the dean's office and my lunch hours eating with the kids in the student cafeteria. The kids knew me as "Rod" and responded well to my approach, which combined effective listening, empathy, clear communication and toughness.

I knew the Boys' Dean was going to move on, so I applied for the position. Our new principal, Margaret Baird, was the first African American high school principal in NYC. I remember walking into her office and telling her of my intentions. At first, she warmly laughed and asked me two things. Had I looked in the mirror, and had I checked my birth certificate? I sold her on the reputation I had garnered with the students during my volunteering experience and laid out a plan to get heroin out of the school, which was an insidious out-of-control problem.

In those days, pure heroin was sold in what was called "nickel bags" ($5.00), and we had an epidemic of students hooked on it. My plan was to change the nature of the dean's office from being strictly disciplinary, to an office that combined necessary discipline with a consultative approach, including input from the students. The plan also included "strip searching" students (doing a complete search of the body down to their underwear) when they were suspected of carrying heroin, and, if drugs were found, placing them under arrest into the Rockefeller Program, where they would be treated for their addiction, then released. This was a lot to take in for Margaret, so she brought in the head of the Parent-Teacher Association for consultation. After laying out the plan, they both gave me a conditional six-month approval. I did this all instinctively because I was not as clearly conscious back then of how change and growth worked.

As I took on the role, I found many allies to my approach. In fact, the students who wanted heroin out of the school became an important support, as they would notify me of drug deals going down so we could intervene.

Sometimes, when I ate lunch with the kids, I would purposely choose to sit at a table where a suspected dealer was sitting. I would get around to the subject of drugs, then acknowledge the dealer to their friends at the table by lightheartedly mentioning how this guy kept beating me. The "dealer" would always deny it; however I would let him know that as much as he had won in the past, there would come a day when I would catch him and perform a strip search and, if he was holding, have him arrested. I then would shake his hand and ask him to agree that if that occurred, there would be no hard feelings. They almost always shook my hand. Amazingly, in my numerous encounters in catching student dealers, never once did they turn on me, because of the open and honest conversations we'd had previously. I would simply remind them of our earlier conversations and that "this is that time we talked about earlier when we shook hands".

Things were changing. Not only was I going through my own shift in consciousness and eliminating limited belief systems, but I was able to shift the consciousness of the school administrators and students.

One day, some fellow teachers started a unique program called the "Love Project". Its core emphasis was that every one of us has a natural desire to contribute to others when given the invitation and the opportunity to do it. Our students had never been exposed to anything like this, and it took off like wildfire, garnering national attention. San Diego State's Graduate Education Department came to Jefferson and spent a week observing the success of the program and then invited a group of teachers and students to come to their program (The National Center for the Exploration of Human Potentialities) and learn how to run encounter groups based on Carl Rogers' self-actualization approach. It was the summer of 1971, and a group of us—including Margaret Baird, our principal, other teachers and students—went to San Diego and dove into the training. We brought it back to Jefferson with enormous success.

When I look back at my final days in Brooklyn and my first days in San Diego, I can acknowledge now that it was the end of the beginning of my transformation. It had started with Renna insisting I had the power to change my life and challenge the beliefs that had been poured into me. It ended when I closed the chapter of my life in New York and started a new one in San Diego, California.

In San Diego, I got a teaching license and made every effort to get into teaching. Jobs were slim that year, so I turned my focus to the uncharted waters of the business world, which I knew nothing about. What I didn't know then was this would usher in the second wave of my personal transformation. My prior role, in education, came to me naturally, as I was in alignment with some core beliefs poured into me by thriving on creating opportunities (dare I say WOW moments) for growth both within me and in the student community. I was part of that community and was empowered to make change happen. Now I was in an entirely new arena, and I was scared and felt ill equipped.

———

FINAL THOUGHTS
Who Are You?

Before we leave this chapter on Overcoming Limited Beliefs, it's important to examine Who Are You? This is an enormously important question that anyone in a relationship with you (professionally, socially or intimately) might want to know. How often do you check in with yourself and ask this very question? I have found that by asking myself "**who am I becoming**?" I get clearer about understanding who I am, what I believe and what I stand for. Between the crevices, I get to see what got poured into me. It is not always obvious; however, if you are willing and open, your inner beliefs will appear.

Imagine for a moment that your results in your life are based upon your consciousness (your inner beliefs).

If this is true, can you see how limiting it can be if you have an inner belief that says, "I'm not smart enough, or I couldn't see myself that successful, or that people with money are materialistic and greedy"? How the hell, in that last example, would your mind ever allow you to be successful financially if your inner belief painted a picture of materialism and greed associated with success? The mind, with its preordained beliefs, will fight like hell to keep you the same and justify, through righteousness, your status quo. It will make people with money wrong in your mind simply to keep that status quo. The caution here is not to get caught up doing the same thing over and over again, expecting a different result (paraphrasing Einstein).

I encourage you to spend time reflecting on the inherited elements in your glass that comprise the operating system that runs your beliefs, opinions and results in your life. I want to be clear that we all have free will, and that at any given time we, as humans, truly do step up and create great results out of sheer will and desire. However, it is a harsh reality that masses of people wallow in the latest political news, the latest health issue, the latest news report, the latest Dow Jones, the latest celebrity crisis, the latest gossip, the latest economic news, the latest disagreement in your relationship, etc., which affects our mood for the day. We leave in the dust our genetically and spiritually entrenched right to declare our joy and create our own happiness.

In my experience, finding your authentic self is a worthy quest and will attract a more fulfilled life. By the way, nothing is wrong with the status quo if that is what you want; remember, it's all a choice.

FIVE
MONEY CONSCIOUSNESS

S ince expanding my money consciousness has been the driver of my success, I'd thought I'd share what contributed to my makeup and what led to my many successes.

———

LOVE COMES KNOCKING

My story of money consciousness would not have been what it is without one person, and that is my wife, Jeri. It's funny to say, but our story began years before we even met. She was eighteen, living in San Diego, California, and I was nineteen, living in Brooklyn, New York. Unbeknownst to either of us, we both independently had a defining memory that, we believe, was a precursor to our attraction.

I still recall it as if it were yesterday. I was lying on a park bench in Brooklyn, looking at the stars and imagining how my life would unfold. The whole world seemed quiet as I had this enlightening thought that the love of my life was out there somewhere. My only clue was that she was a strong, independent woman very different from my then current circumstance of being in a committed relationship with a very dependent girlfriend that started when I was fourteen.

About the same time period in San Diego, Jeri had a definitive moment when it occurred to her that the man she would marry was already on the planet. She envisioned a dark-haired man on the east coast (she had never been there), studying in college. It wasn't until we were together that it occurred to her that I was that guy she had envisioned when she was eighteen years old.

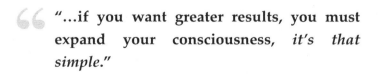

"...if you want greater results, you must expand your consciousness, *it's that simple.*"

Let's roll forward to 1978. I had spent the previous nine

years recreating my life's view while participating in personal growth work with a keen focus on "looking within" for my answers. I was in a great spiritual space; however, I was economically struggling while being a single parent to my sons, Dan and Tyler, from my second marriage, and living in a rented room with a mattress on the floor. Yeah, that's how bad my money consciousness was.

One day, my boys and I went to a park. I had inadvertently dropped my jacket on the ground, and this beautiful woman went over and picked it up. As it turned out, this was to be my future sister-in-law, Judy, who also had two little children, Tahnee and Neal. Judy and I lightly dated and mostly enjoyed doing things with our kids. One day she invited me to join her, with the kids, at the Circus Vargas traveling circus. When I got there, I was introduced to her sister Jeri. Turned out that Jeri and I were in alignment on our passion for personal growth, and we spent an hour having a really enlightened conversation. At that time, I was interested in Judy, so there was no further interest in Jeri past this conversation. Ultimately, my relationship with Judy transformed into a light friendship.

About a year later, I attended a party, and Jeri spotted me in the kitchen and told me I looked familiar. After a moment I realized who she was. We talked for a bit; then she mentioned she was there with someone and should get back to him. A bit later, I was walking through the party and saw Jeri standing with a guy, who I assumed was the one she'd invited.

Jeri had come to the party in hopes of meeting other successful women and had invited a gentleman, I'll call him Robert, who was going through a divorce, to see if he could meet women. I didn't know that information; however, the conversation came around to Robert speaking about his soon-to-be ex-wife. He was quite negative, so I shared with him some different perspectives on the situation, as I clearly had experience there. I would say things like "the way to have what you want in your life is to support her having what she wants in her life" and that letting go of "being right" would be a key to his happiness. Robert didn't seem to be enjoying what I was sharing.

I left for the bathroom, and Robert turned to Jeri and said, "What an asshole." Unbeknownst to me, Jeri was resonating with every word that came out of my mouth and already expressing gratitude to the Universe for bringing me to her. When I returned, Robert dug in and kept challenging my views. Each time he got amped, I got calmer and responded with more challenging concepts. It was then I sensed that Jeri was connecting with me, which inspired me to get even more enthused about sharing with Robert. In essence, it was like an incredible date/interview where she got to see who I am without asking me a question. I could literally feel her next to me without touching. Suddenly, Robert excused himself to go to the bathroom. My whole spirit was alive; I turned to Jeri, looked her in the eyes and said, "This is crazy, Jeri, I just love you." Jeri in turn said, "I love you too." We hugged and have never let go of each other since that moment.

There are many reasons to love Jeri; however, I'd be remiss if I didn't mention how she not only embraced me as a man and husband but also embraced Dan, Kym and Tyler as her own children. None were her blood, yet she opened her arms and her home as if they were and became their mom.

———

Second Epiphany Day

Are you willing to save a $3,000 day?

Have you ever wondered why you don't seem to get what you think you want in your life? The answer is amazingly simple, and the answer teaches us the most fundamental thing we need to know and experience about consciousness. The answer is found in the saying **"We attract to ourselves at the level of our consciousness"**. You and I are getting results based upon the consciousness that *preceded* the results. **So, if you want**

greater results, you must expand your consciousness, *it's that simple.*

You might ask, how do I do that? You do that by looking inside and not outside yourself for the answer. The answer will unfold when you are willing to leave all beliefs and assumptions at the door, be open to new thought, be vulnerable, get out of your head, and be in true partnership with Infinite Intelligence. Worth repeating, be willing to leave all beliefs and assumptions at the door, be open to new thought, be vulnerable, get out of your head, and *be in true partnership with Infinite Intelligence.*

Before I share with you my journey to a $3,000 day, I want you to be clear that regardless of what your spouse, your parents, your friends or I may want, there is no requirement for you to change your consciousness. Life and your results are simply a choice, and you alone are the one who waves your magic wand. Be at peace with yourself and accept the results of your consciousness gracefully. Don't beat yourself up, don't blame others, and don't be in resistance to the results. Accept that most of your results come from your inherited consciousness and are exactly the way the results were co-created based on beliefs that got poured into you as a child, when you had no vote and no veto.

This is a lot to take in, so I would suggest taking a moment to read over these first two paragraphs, close your eyes and ponder these concepts as well as asking yourself the following:

- Are you willing to stop blaming others for your results?
- Are you willing to stop blaming *yourself* for your results?
- Are you willing to accept that the results you created are exactly in harmony with your consciousness that preceded them?
- Are you willing to grow, even if you are not sure how to do it?

It's very important to ponder these questions before hearing from me about a personal journey through consciousness that was so powerful, real and measurable.

When I was a kid in Brooklyn, NY, I was a baseball pitcher with average physical ability, yet I consistently had above average results. Looking back, I realize now that I was tapping into a very high level of consciousness that affected my results. Before every game while warming up, I would assess how I was doing. Was I accurate that day, did I have good speed that day, did my arm feel good, etc.? If I was not my best in warm-ups, I would consciously accept that I may not have my best stuff that day. Then I would think quietly about the results I wanted and harness my willingness to create great results in the midst of my less than best ability that day. Amazingly to some and not to me, I would create great results and win. I knew as a kid that in sports, if I was willing to have great results, then typically I would. So one would think that if I was good at mastering this consciousness on the playing field, certainly I would master it in all areas of my life. Well, was I surprised when I entered the world of business, where income is a direct measurement of your money consciousness.

Let's jump forward to early 1979. I was thirty-two years old and in copier sales in San Diego County, CA. Having primary custody and responsibility for my two sons, Dan and Tyler, from my previous marriage, I was single and driving a beat-up Pontiac Sunbird and renting a room in a house where my sons and I slept on a mattress on the floor. In the midst of this measurable money consciousness, I met Jeri, a beautiful woman and successful Realtor making almost six times more than the $20,000 a year I had made in commissions that year.

Jeri was clear that she could only count on herself to eat and be successful. As a result, she had decided she would give herself everything a man would give her and set up camp on her dream horse ranch in East San Diego County. Amazingly and thankfully, Jeri was able to look beyond my money consciousness and see that my consciousness in other areas, especially in personal accountability, appeared quite advanced. With that comfort, Jeri invited my sons, me and our dog, Jenny, to move into her home. This is where a wonderful journey full of challenges and growth took flight.

After moving in, it became painfully obvious to me, as a man, that Jeri did not need me for her success. Jeri was tough; she grew up with a dad who was highly successful and one of the founders of Fedmart, a company created by Sol Price (Price Club). He was everything a little girl would want in a dad. Unfortunately, at twelve years old, she lost her beloved daddy in a plane crash, leaving her with her mother, who suffered from alcoholism. As a result, she learned only to count on herself for everything.

{If you are interested, Jeri wrote a bestseller called *Where's the Love and Who's Got My Money?* sharing her life story and her growth through consciousness. Available on Amazon.}

It also became obvious to me that this tough, business-minded woman had a little girl inside dying to get out, if only it was safe. I knew that this woman was a key to my happiness, in every area, and I knew I might learn a thing or two about money consciousness if I was a willing student. Finally, I knew that regardless of my then current financial status, I had a great and honest love to share with her that would richly fill her heart. As the saying goes, "Good trade."

In the copier business I was a foot soldier, working the front lines selling machines. I was given a territory, a gurney-type cart and a pat on the behind, well, not literally. Many days consisted of going door-to-door, meeting receptionist after receptionist, whose job was to screen salespeople, take a card and say the magic words: "We'll give you a call if something comes up." This process was brutal to my spirit, especially because I had been very successful in education in New York City. While my relationship with Jeri was growing in so many ways, my relationship with my money consciousness, i.e., myself, was not doing so great.

Jeri and I had participated in EST, a series of personal growth seminars, and one night on the way home from one, I shared how frustrated I was with myself in the copier business. My thoughts were that I should find another career because I certainly wasn't enjoying the rejections to my efforts. Jeri wasn't buying it, pulled the car into a parking lot, turned the ignition off and asked me if I wanted to handle my money case right now. My response was a resounding yes.

What I am about to share with you, while appearing to be about me, is really about a spiritual process where fundamental internal principles are at work, principles that we all have access to within ourselves. What's so powerful about this example is the speed with which new thought created new form. Pay attention, relate it to you, and enjoy the journey.

———————

My $3,000 day
(Master Breakthrough in My Money Consciousness)

So here we are sitting in a parking lot, with nowhere to hide, challenging myself to be vulnerable and expose my true thoughts. Little did I know I was in for a three-hour crash course in money consciousness. When you hear the entire story and especially the results, you will realize the phenomenal and life-changing return on investment for those three hours.

Jeri started by presenting a scenario to me. She knew I loved visualization, so she described a scene where I am driving and pull up to a stoplight and a Mercedes convertible pulls up next to me. In the Mercedes is a woman with diamond jewelry on her wrist, neck, ears and fingers. To stimulate me even more, she went on to describe her white toy poodle, whose collar and leash were sparkling in diamonds, as well. Well before Jeri asked me the question, I already was in judgment about the excesses. Jeri then asked me what I thought of the woman. My response was instantaneous, that this woman was materialistic. Jeri pointed out that my face had changed as though in pain, and asked me how I was feeling. I indicated that I actually felt disgust. She said, "Great," and added another scenario. A man pulls up next to me in a Rolls Royce, smoking a cigar. The man has a Rolex and a gold chain around his neck. Again, my reaction was that he is materialistic. Jeri pointed out that, in each case, when someone appeared to have money, I judged them as being materialistic, I reacted and obviously *did not want to be like them.* She nailed it right on the head.

Then came the magic moment of discovery as Jeri pointed out a principle that was at work here. Because I disdained what looked like money, every time I moved towards having money, the money would move away at the same speed because, fundamentally, I did not want to be what it looked like. I DID NOT WANT TO BE MATERIALISTIC. My reaction was so automatic and lacking in conscious reason or thought. It became so obvious that what got poured into me as a child was at work here. Noticing this, I got really excited, and we dug deeper and discovered I had a belief that if you had money, you would be inclined to be less loving, the opposite of what I prided myself on being. Bottom line was that I realized my SubConscious beliefs would fight like hell to keep the status quo, and I would never have significant money in my life if I continued to allow my inherited limiting beliefs to dominate my thought.

Now my curiosity was on fire, and I asked Jeri how to

overcome these thoughts that had been poured into me. She replied that I had to create new thought to replace them. Jeri suggested that I *bless people you perceive to have money*. Think well of them, and when you are with someone who has attracted money in their life, say "good for you". I tried it on, thought of someone I knew personally with money, blessed them and noticed a favorable shift in my consciousness, seeing him in a different light. Jeri pointed out to me an incredible principle that *"until you can bless others for their good fortune, you will not attract it into your life"*.

[Take a moment and think about the process I went through and ask yourself about your response to the woman and her toy poodle with the diamonds and the man in the Rolls Royce. Notice your thoughts. Can you see yourself in the Rolls Royce? Think of someone you know with money. What inner talk do you have about him/her? If negative, choose to bless them.]

With such a discovery, I thought I was done; however, Jeri had other things in mind for me. She asked me if I really wanted to dig in and get to work on my new thought. My response was an enthusiastic yes, and we began another journey, which took two of the three hours to complete.

Jeri asked me a simple question that was easy for me to relate to. She asked me: "How much money do you want to make in a month?" After some reflection, I answered $3,000. Jeri asked me why $3,000. I told her I was making about $1,700 a month in commissions and that my true overhead was about $2,000. If I made $3,000, I would have an excess of $1,000 and, more importantly, could take her (Jeri) to a restaurant and not feel the bill. What I didn't tell her at the time was that it would also make me feel more like a man. Jeri pressed on and asked me if $3,000 was real for me and could I own it, and could I actually feel it and commit to making $3,000 a month, even this month with two weeks left. I said yes emphatically.

Now came the reality check. Jeri then asked me if I was *willing* to have it happen. My mind froze, and I asked her, rhetorically, what did willingness have to do with this? I went on to educate Jeri that she didn't understand the copier business. You need a strong sales pipeline, mine wasn't, and with two weeks left and a bad sales territory, it couldn't happen. Boy, did I feel reasonable and "right" with my answer, and I continued until Jeri told me to stop.

She asked me again how much money I wanted each month and to explain my reasoning for choosing $3,000 and what that $1,000 extra each month would mean to me. Again, I imagined taking her to a restaurant and not feeling the bill. This part was real for me. But then she got right back to the nitty-gritty of my consciousness. "Is the $3,000 real for you, can you feel it, can you own it, and are you willing to have this happen?" Again, I repeated the obvious that I had no copier deals working and that she didn't understand the realities of the copier world, and besides, there were only two weeks left in this month, and no way was that enough time to pull it off.

I'd like to take a diversion here for a moment. Years ago, an author by the name of Richard Bach wrote a wonderful story about individual freedom called *Jonathan Livingston Seagull*. Neil Diamond the singer made it into an album, and a movie was created based on the book. Richard's next book was called *Illusions: A Handbook for a Reluctant Messiah*, basically you and I being the reluctant messiah in our lives. Throughout the book there are powerful and poignant sayings that strike a chord in our consciousness. Given what I just shared with you about my reasoning for *not being able* to create $3,000 that month, it might help to hear Richard speaking to each of us. *"Argue for your limitations and sure enough they are yours."*

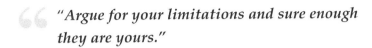

> *"Argue for your limitations and sure enough they are yours."*

Still in the car and the parking lot, Jeri shared with me other concepts about how we attract to our life where we are coming from in consciousness and we repel that which we are not in harmony with. Round and round we went, going through the same exercise about what I wanted, why, and was I willing for it to happen. Finally, after three hours, my mind "ran out of material" and the limiting arguments inside me went quiet. I answered a resounding YES to my willingness to have it happen. Jeri turned the ignition on, and we drove home in silence. I noticed my mind was absolutely at peace and there was no self-talk going on. I slept like a baby that night.

Jeri always shared this quote with me: "*If you are praying for potatoes, reach for a hoe.*" The next morning, I reached for that hoe and went to work. Something was very different for me. I noticed how everyone and everything seemed more alive, and I was excited to be in the office. I had just sat down at my desk when a note was passed to me that, at 9:07 a.m., Grossmont Bank, in my territory, had called and asked me to contact them today. I called immediately, and they told me they remembered me and I had been in six months earlier and they were ready to replace some copiers. I went out there and sold them two copiers worth about $2,000 in commission.

Later that day, I went back to the office to do the paperwork and another call came in from my territory. This one was what we in sales call a "blue bird" because it was totally unexpected and out of the blue. I had never called on them before. I went out, demonstrated a copier and walked away with a sale worth about $700 in commission.

At the end of the day, I was driving home thinking with excitement how I couldn't wait to tell Jeri I had made $2,700 in just one day. Then this voice deep inside me said: "Wouldn't it have been great if I had made $3,000 that day?" It was an old familiar voice with the obvious inflection that not only did I not make it happen (failure) but that it couldn't happen. Good old inherited limited thinking. I chose, at that moment, to make a stand and told the voice inside my mind, in strong words not suitable to print, to "shut up".

I looked around and saw a building, parked the car and walked up to an architects' office. I saw a woman with a purse over her shoulder at the door locking up. I presented her with the hard truth that I was in the copier business and it was 4:55 p.m. on a Friday night and it was the worst time to call on her. She looked at me incredulously and said, "I can't believe you are here right now. That copier (pointing through the window) broke down for the third time this week, and my boss said to replace it." She told me they do about ten copies per day and then asked me if I could come back on Monday. I said, "Absolutely and if you are willing to stay another fifteen minutes, I have a copier in my car that might fit your needs." She agreed, and lo and behold, she bought the copier right off my cart.

As I got in my car, I took out the paperwork and calculated that this sale gave me a commission of $400, which meant I made $3,100 in one day. I sat and pondered what had just happened over the past twenty-four hours. I realized that, when I was *willing* to get beyond my internal limiting thoughts, life opened up. Instead of a big "woohoo", a calm came over me as I realized what I had just witnessed was a spiritual process at work within me. I felt humble and grateful that I was blessed with this gift to partner with the Infinite Intelligence. When I got home and wrapped my loving arms around Jeri, I shared quietly about the events of the day and my newfound awareness. It was a very special moment that Jeri and I will always remember, for it was the beginning of a new era in thought and growth for me.

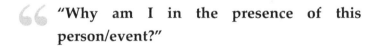 **"Why am I in the presence of this person/event?"**

Following that moment,

I never again could deny the connection between my thoughts (prayers) and the results in my life. What was so great about what happened was that the shift in consciousness was so specific and so measurable. Never once did I think it was a fluke, and I went on a journey of growth in which I continually would find myself again telling that old voice in my mind to shut up. An integral thought in my journey was to trust whatever God/Universe put in front of me. I learned how to ask myself, **"Why am I in the presence of this person/event?"** That question has permeated my approach to everything life put in front of me and has opened so many new doors.

The wonderful update to my $3,000 day took place in early 2002 while Jeri and I were in our CPA's office discussing our taxes. By the way, for me, my success is never about the money but more about getting beyond limited thinking, creating and bringing value to the world. Jeri always handled our finances, and I was typically unaware of how much money I earned. In the middle of the meeting, Jeri pushed a piece of paper my way with a dollar amount that reflected my income for 2001. She asked me to divide that number by 365 days. I was humbled and grateful as I pressed the equal key to see that, for 2001, I had earned **$3,000 a day**, every day that year. I looked at Jeri with a loving and grateful smile (and some tears) and quietly thanked God/Universe for the blessings that my partnership with the Infinite Intelligence had co-created.

––––––

An Ongoing Process (A Horse Named Blake)

I must tell you now that consciousness is an ongoing

process. The lessons are not something you do once and then go about the rest of your life. In fact, it is an everyday thing. Consider it a shift in the way you think, much like you do when you alter your diet to a lifestyle change. You'll still encounter those limited beliefs coming back, but when they do, you'll be equipped to handle them promptly and shift your thinking.

It was the early nineties and we were growing our young business, pouring every available dollar back into it. At the same time, my wife, Jeri, was an avid equestrian who was challenging herself by competing in the hunter/jumper circuit. In order to compete at that level, she needed an experienced horse, so she set out looking for one. I had a great desire to get her what she needed and was not prepared for the reaction I would have when she found the horse of her dreams.

It was a relaxed Sunday morning, and while in bed, Jeri leaned over and told me she had found a horse that would be perfect for her to go forward in her hunter/jumper career. My immediate response: "How much does he cost?" She answered calmly, "Twelve thousand dollars."

For me, $12,000 was like her asking for $100,000, because we didn't just have it lying around. I literally couldn't breathe; it was as if I were being strangled. I gasped for air, got up and walked outside, my hand clutching my chest. I could feel my heart pounding, and my breath still hadn't returned; in fact, it felt as if I were breathing through a straw, a small cocktail straw. As I paced back and forth, I realized I was having a panic attack. Jeri came to me and said, "Rod, forget it. It's not worth it." I replied, "I can't forget it because I know you won't." Given my reaction, we dropped the subject, and Jeri never brought it up again.

True to my word, I could not forget it. Fortunately for me I had trained myself to always look within for my answers. I saw how limited my view was and that my severe reaction was simply due to an inherited belief, one that said I was not worthy or capable of owning such a horse, topped by fear of losing what I had gained so far in the business. I kept looking and looking and finally saw clearly that I needed to up my game and see a bigger, more expanded vision for our business. It was one of those pivotal moments in my journey where I took an internal challenge and chose to grow from it. Believe me, this was a tough one. However, at the end of the day I decided to let my mind know that I was in charge here and for it to shut up.

What happened next was one of the most joyous and grateful moments I had with my beautiful Jeri. A few days had passed since that Sunday morning and my panic attack. I approached her at her desk. She was on the phone and looked up at me towering over her. She gave me a smile and kept talking, but I didn't move. She kept looking at me, no doubt wondering why I was standing there. Finally, her call ended, and she asked me, "What's up?" I reached into my jacket pocket, pulled out a check for $12,000 and handed it to her. I said, "Go buy Blake." Shocked, mainly because of my severe reaction earlier, she kept staring at the check. She looked up with her beautiful eyes and asked, "Are you sure?" Without hesitation, I answered, "I will just make more money." And you know what, I did.

Some basic questions about your money consciousness

If you want to expand your money consciousness, it's essential to understand the inherited beliefs that are in your soil. For example:

1. What do you believe about money?
2. What did your parents say about people with money?
3. How much cash in your pocket would make you uncomfortable and why?

We could go on and on. I have added a very effective questionnaire at the end of this book that will help you explore what is in your soil.

SIX

ALIGNING YOUR BELIEFS WITH YOUR VISION

W*hat's the vision for your life? Do you even have a vision? Why have a vision for your life? What does vision actually mean?*

Let's start with what vision means in the context of having what you want for your life. One definition that rings true for me is **"the ability to think about or plan the future with imagination or wisdom"**. Imagination is the accelerant for your thoughts. I have included below my entrepreneurial journey to illustrate the importance of aligning your beliefs with your vision.

MY ENTREPRENEURIAL BUSINESS JOURNEY

What I am about to share emphasizes the importance of

being open and vigilant to what life presents to you. To do this, it is important to start with believing you are worthy of these opportunities and take immediate action when they present themselves.

In 1975, I was working in the electronic calculator market at a time when we were moving from electro-mechanical gear-driven calculators to electronic calculators using a dot matrix printer (pins). I was working for Victor, one of the leaders in the space. Victor had just come out with a programmable calculator that used magnetic card media to store the data. The machine had no window, just a keyboard.

One day, I walked into the Financial Aid Department of UCSD (University of California San Diego) and observed tax return information being used as part of the basis for determining eligibility for financial aid grants. As I watched, my imagination went to work, as I could see in my mind the calculator doing the calculations automatically. You're reading this and thinking that's not a big thing, but in 1975 it was. What did I immediately do with this idea? Well, I took action. I mentioned to the manager that I had an idea about a new calculator that might be able to perform the calculations automatically. She was intrigued and spent hours with me, taking me through their step-by-step processes.

Fortunately, Victor had just hired its first programmer in San Diego, and I brought this project to him. It took about three months, and we presented the solution to UCSD. They loved it and purchased multiple machines. I then was instructed to create a vertical market specializing in financial aid, and took this solution to other colleges in the San Diego area with similar success. Victor saw the opportunity and expanded the solution nationwide.

There are two lessons here. First, I only got credit for my sales in the San Diego area, even though I had come up with the idea and helped see it through. This is understandable, as Victor had every right not to include me in their national sales, so I made a mental note that if I were ever to come up with another great idea, I would focus on how I would protect my thoughts and be in control of the results. Second, I proved that imagination followed up with immediate action leads to results. This was valuable, and I continued to leverage my mind and imagination going forward, as you'll see.

THE DAWN OF WALZ CERTIFIED MAIL AUTOMATION

When there is a foreclosure of residential property, it is not the lender that actually does the foreclosure processing. Depending on state law, it is either referred to an attorney or referred to a trustee who manages the fore-closure.

In 1982, Nick Francis, a foreclosure trustee in Vista, CA, had an idea on how to use the new microprocessor technology to automate the tedious process of handling foreclosures. Mind you, the technology consisted of a microprocessor in a box that contained a 10MB hard disk, 64k RAM, three terminal ports, one printer port and an eight-inch floppy disk for backups. Up until then, everything for a foreclosure was done on typewriters, and the same documents had to be typed over and over for everyone attached to a foreclosable property.

Nick hired a programmer (not the programmer from Victor) whom I had met during my days at Victor. Together they created the software and matched it to a microprocessor. They needed someone to take it to the streets and sell this solution. The programmer thought of me, and at the same time, I was searching to find him to help with some research I was doing. We found each other and I got excited about this new solution. I joined the team as VP of Sales. Being a new company, it had its issues, and a year later some partners and I bought the company and moved it to the Los Angeles area as a subset in another business the partners owned.

Part of the foreclosure process includes sending Notice of Defaults and other associated documents simultaneously by Certified Mail and First-Class Mail to delinquent borrowers. If you've ever had to send something by Certified Mail, you know how tedious filling out each of the forms is. The software, very smartly, led the user in a prescribed order of entry, printing on the USPS Certified Mail and Return Receipt forms. The clients were ecstatic, and I remember the first time I demonstrated it to a potential client and watched their "wow" expression envelop their face as they realized they only had to put the data in once.

After about a year, I realized the luster of the rudimentary Certified Mail feature might wear off and began looking for a form set that could be used in place of the USPS-provided forms. I found none, so one night, I placed tissue paper on a glass table with a portable lamp underneath and created a multiple part continuous form set that contained two stacked addressee inserts for the Certified and First-Class mail envelopes along with stacked Certified Mail and Return Receipt forms. I then had Moore Business Forms manufacture the forms set. However, before that could be done, I had to get USPS approval for the design to privately print the USPS forms, which required some adjusting of fields. I eventually spoke with USPS headquarters and presented my idea. At first, they said no. But with my **persistence** that this solution made it easy to prepare Certified Mail, they embraced my vision and approved the design.

My vision, at the time, was small and limited to just

being used with our foreclosure system. My partners wanted to focus on other business, so I horse-traded a sales commission and purchased the rights to all the assets involving the foreclosure system, including the Certified Mail designs.

Jeri and I lived in the east county of San Diego, and most of my sales focus was in the Los Angeles area. This required long two-to-three-hour drives up and down. On a particular Friday, before I started my trek home through LA traffic, I went to a pay phone and called Jeri to tell her I was leaving, and traffic looked bad. Before I got off the phone, Jeri mentioned that we had received an earthquake insurance solicitation by Certified Mail. I hung up, got in the car and began my tedious trek home in ten-mile-per-hour traffic, all the while intrigued by what Jeri had told me about the Certified Mail we'd just received. I remember asking myself, why was I in the presence of this information Jeri shared? I soon had my answer.

I let my imagination run and then it came. What if what I had invented for Certified Mail could be used all over the country in different industries? I went on to imagine people using the forms and telling others about how great they were. To bring my vision to life, I used various accents to accentuate the vision. I saw the forms being used in Brooklyn and imagined people using them, then telling others. Brooklyn accent: "Hey, Joey, look at these forms." Dallas accent: "Hey, Betty Jane, y'all gotta see this." San Diego accent: "Hey, dude, check this out."

I was so excited about what my vision was showing me that I pulled off the freeway and called Jeri again. I asked her if we would be alone that night (we had house guests at the time). She said we could be, and asked me why. I told her I needed to talk with her alone, then hung up. Because of the anxious tone in my voice, Jeri was curious and even imagined that maybe the poor boy had gone astray and needed to fess up. When I got home, I was beyond excited and had Jeri follow me to the bedroom. After I closed the door, I opened my briefcase and removed a stack of the Certified Mail forms I had created, then shared my nationwide vision with her. She chuckled and asked if this was what I wanted to talk about "alone"? I said yes, and she laughingly explained how she had imagined I had gone astray.

We remembered my time at Victor regarding intellectual property and set out to find an attorney, John Haller, to see if we could get my idea patented. Our first patent was issued in November 1987. Subsequently, we invested in patent insurance to ward off infringers, which proved effective ten times in our first year.

It was now time to give the form a name. I came up with various combinations of Certified Form Solutions, etc. We met with John Haller and he asked us why we didn't include our name, Walz, in the product name. I explained that we were taking this nationally and didn't want to appear small. *The truth was that my vision was not big enough.* He challenged us with our own thinking and vision. He encouraged us to visualize ten years from now and see the "Walz" brand everywhere. We followed his advice and branded the form as the "WALZ Certified Mailer". Boy, was John Haller right. Since its inception, the WALZ Certified Mailer has been used in close to 300,000,000 transactions, resulting in millions of hours of time savings for clients as well as Walz becoming a household name in the USPS and the mailing industry. This anchor product became the financial cornerstone for what new Walz products and services were to come.

One of the important takeaways from this experience was the importance of taking *immediate action* on your vision. We didn't hesitate to move forward and find a patent attorney and prepare for life after the patent. With growth, fear inevitably shows up. So whenever we did something new, *we welcomed fear* and embraced it as a sign that we were growing. It's really important to examine the fear and see what is real while also seeing what is based on your inherited limited thinking.

I'd be remiss not to share my gratitude for John Haller. He was key to our success, specifically with his insistence on using our name, Walz, as the brand, which carried over into multiple products and services beyond just Certified Mail.

————

WALZ Item Tracking System (WITS)

In 1990, I was deep in the throes of marketing our Certified Mail automation nationally and was making a presentation about using our automation (software and forms), in front of fourteen mail center managers at Chemical Bank in New York. About twenty minutes into my presentation, another invitee came huffing and puffing through the door, telling us how bad the traffic was on the Long Island Expressway. As it turned out, his interest was not in outbound Certified Mail. He was responsible for receiving all the inbound Certified Mail for the entire bank; however, I was not aware of that.

After a few moments, he realized what we were talking about was not relevant to his needs. In a brash New York voice, he blurted out his annoyance at being there and called me out as a "g--damned salesman from California". I replied that I was from Brooklyn and went to Xaverian High School and St. John's University. He then asked me if I knew Frank DelMonico, who went to Xaverian, and I indicated that we'd played basketball often back then. After knowing a bit about my background, he calmed down.

At this time in my life, I had gotten into the habit of asking *"Why am I in the presence of what's in front of me?"* so, after my presentation, I asked him about what he did with inbound Certified Mail, and he proceeded to tell me about sorting the mail by routes through the city and hand logging them for signature. Like the earthquake insurance Certified Mail, I was intrigued, and because I had gotten into the practice, I let my imagination run with it.

As I was flying home, my head was spinning with ideas. What if I could reverse engineer *outbound* Certified Mail to be an *inbound* system? Back home, I got together with my programmers and in six months developed the WALZ Item Tracking System (WITS), which took off like wildfire as the first system to track accountable mail, FedEx and UPS packages. Upon further thinking, we expanded our vision beyond just the initial thoughts and evolved it to **track anything**. FedEx in their Memphis headquarter sites and the USPS headquarters in Washington, DC, used it on their docks to track all their inbound items, a large federal agency used it to track secrets and secured print jobs, HP used it to track gas cylinders, and so on and so on. WITS was the cornerstone for the tracking industry that followed.

The lesson here is that life will bring you the opportunities if you are open to them. Imagine if I had just said sorry to the Chemical Bank guy for the misunderstanding and never inquired what his needs were. Always ask, *"Why am I in the presence of what's in front of me?"* You will be amazed at how much there is available to you.

———

LETTING MY VISION AND IMAGINATION LEAD THE WAY

It's 2001, and I was in full appreciation and gratitude for our success with Certified Mail and our WITS automation, but like I said about money consciousness, the work is never done. You must always be working to improve by challenging yourself. One way I do this is by asking myself the question *"Who Am I Becoming?"* which usually results in me asking, *"What's next?"*

By this time many large lenders were using the WALZ Certified Mailers for their delinquency mailings, which asked for payment and warned them of impending foreclosure action. I had a thought about what it would mean to them if they outsourced their critical mailings to WALZ. Would it be an added value for them? Would they become more efficient? Mind you, we had no idea if we could really perform.

Countrywide Home Loans was one of our clients with the WALZ Certified Mailers. I set up an exploratory meeting and they gave me a golden pass to talk to all the internal staff dealing with their delinquency notices that they handled in-house. The research showed that it would be of significant value to lenders handling delinquencies; now we just needed to pull it off.

My *thought and vision* of adding significant value was validated. I convened with our staff, led by an incredibly creative employee and dear friend, Robyn Arreola. It took six months for Robyn to work with our programmers in modifying our then current WALZ Postal Software to create a rudimentary solution for outsourcing. Finally, a WALZ Certified Mailer lender customer chose in and outsourced their work to us successfully.

It didn't take long to realize that producing the mailing and the notices wasn't the leading value proposition. As we poured through the delinquency letter templates, we saw legacy issues with the wording. For example, we found a Spanish version that said "You will get fees from a reasonable attorney" rather than "reasonable attorney fees". We discovered incomplete sentences, etc. It was then we realized the real value we offered was being a neutral third party with eyes upon the accuracy of the documents. We set our vision on becoming the pre-eminent compliance technology company in the mortgage/foreclosure industry, and we pulled it off. At one time, we handled the mailing of approximately 50% of all residential delinquent notices nationally.

All those stories above detail the importance of having a vision, then executing that vision. While it may seem daunting, I can tell you that it's not. Of course, the action part means you have to put the work in; nothing comes from just thinking about what you want, you *MUST ACT*. Achieving things is more than just repeating mantras, affirmations or vision boards (all good). You have to roll up your sleeves and set to the task. Again, as my wife, Jeri, reminds us, *"If you are praying for potatoes, reach for a hoe."*

————

THE VISION FORMULA

You have a thought that you want a bigger and better job or maybe to change your career. *The amazing thing is that you don't even need to know what that job is.* What's more relevant is how you "visualize" your life after you have this new job or change in career.

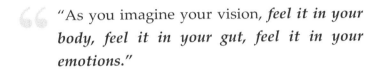

> "As you imagine your vision, *feel it in your body, feel it in your gut, feel it in your emotions."*

———

IMAGINE/SEE IT

Imagine the following:

- How open am I to making a change like this? Very, unlimited, or limited?
- What will be my contribution/my value? Am I making a difference for others, myself, my family?
- How much risk am I willing to take? A lot, cautious, or reasonable?
- What environment will I be working in? Open office, cubicle, indoors, outdoors, or home?
- What is the employment arrangement? Employee, independent contractor, boss, no boss, manager, or team?
- How do I feel in my new position? Challenged, excited?
- Will this new position be near home or away? Nationally, internationally?
- What clothes will I be wearing? Casual, very casual, business, formal?
- What will the people be like at work? Friendly, driven?
- What will my family and friends think about

what I'm doing? Supportive, concerned, excited?

- How will others react to me? Cooperate, respect, or challenge?
- What type of hours will I keep? Short, long, days, or evenings?
- How much free time will I have outside work? Will I care? What works for me?
- What do I think about myself in this new position? Proud, uncomfortable, living my dream?
- How much will I be making? $ range?
- How will I be paid? Commission, salary, both, profits?
- Will I need a car? Personal, corporate?
- Will I have an expense account? Corporate credit card?
- What new friendships will happen in my new job or career? Friends, love interest?
- Etc., etc.

The magic here is in fully imagining all the aspects, in essence a wish list, for your vision. The clearer you are, the better. The Universe now has some very specific elements to include for what it puts before you.

———

FEEL IT

As you imagine your vision, *feel it in your body, feel it in your gut, feel it in your emotions.* These feelings are akin to an accelerant that ignites the creative juices. Living in your head, without the feelings, will limit the opportunities the Universe puts forth. Your body is connected as one with your spirit and is an important element in bringing vision to life.

TAKE IMMEDIATE ACTION

As tricky as this may sound, action *MUST* occur. The action of movement attracts more movement towards your vision; this builds upon itself.

- Start your research in all directions.
- Find and talk with highly successful people. Ask them what their vision has been or is. What roadblocks did they encounter, and how did they get around them? What was the best part of going for their vision?
- Avoid, like a plague, talking with anyone in your circle who wants to stay in the status quo of their lives.

- Know that you are always in connection with your God/Universe and that what was meant to be may reflect your vision or may be something else that you did not envision.
- Enjoy the journey, and if you get blocked along the way, choose again your vision when these obstacles seem to rise up.

Taking Immediate Action Is Really Important. The following are some real examples from my journey:

The first example of taking immediate action revolves around the banking/mortgage industry. There was a period in the late eighties known as the Savings and Loan (S&L) Crisis. It was 1989 and one-third of all savings and loans had failed. At this time, we were looking for new markets to sell our Walz Certified Mailers. It was a Sunday and Jeri and I were sitting on our couch, watching the news. A story came on about how this S&L crisis was severely affecting Texas. In the piece, it showed empty office buildings in Houston followed by a statement that foreclosures were on the rise. As that statement was made, they put up a video of a person filling out a USPS Return Receipt (green card) by hand. Jeri and I couldn't believe our eyes, and we grabbed each other's hand while staring at the television. We looked at each other and agreed this would be our next market.

The following day we purchased a mailing list of

every S&L in Texas. We put together an envelope containing ten samples of our Walz Certified Mailer along with an order form. On the outside of the envelope was a message "Please pass this envelope on to users of Certified Mail". Within days we received order after order, with checks inside, requesting the forms as soon as possible. Usually, when you do a marketing mailing, if you get a 1% response (just being interested), it was considered a win. In this case we got a 9% response *with actual orders*, which was phenomenal. It opened our eyes to having a focused marketing campaign in the banking/mortgage industry, becoming our biggest market.

Another example of taking immediate action happened in the legal industry. It was 1989 and we were exhibiting at our first trade show in the legal industry, known as the Association of Legal Administrators (ALA). The attendees were the people who managed the law firms. Typically they were women who came up through the legal secretary ranks, so they were knowledgeable about all the manual processes facing legal secretaries. Our booth had an effective banner that asked, "Do You Send Certified Mail?" which garnered a lot of interest. It also contained a computer and dot matrix printer for demonstrating how we produce Certified Mail on a centralized basis. Our sales pitch focused on having a centralized workstation where the legal secretaries would bring their requests for Certified Mail. The operator, at that workstation, would enter the names and addresses, print the Walz Certified Mailers and hand them back to the individual legal secretary who had requested them. Even though we had a lot of interest during the first morning, no one seemed ready to buy.

Then it happened. It was lunchtime and I was in my booth. I looked up and saw a woman walking briskly and purposely towards me. She actually pointed at me, indicating she was coming to see me. As she entered our booth, she blurted out how frustrated she was with me because "you do not know how to sell your forms to law firms". She went on to explain that every attorney is his/her own business, and that each had a legal secretary focused on them, and that each had a typewriter. She took one of our forms in hand and told us how the form could be inserted into the typewriter and, in seconds, the forms were ready for use. She also showed us how one of the form parts could be used as a charge-back slip for accounting purposes. I cannot tell you enough the gratitude we had for this woman, and we did something very special for her.

We hid the computer and printer and made a stack of individual forms (from the continuous form stacks), and after lunch, when the show resumed, we pitched the Walz Certified Mailer with the typewriter as its automation, emphasizing the charge-back feature. In fact, we called it "low tech", which they greatly appreciated. The response was overwhelming, with one legal administrator after another bringing back other legal administrators. A recurring quote was "this is the form I was telling you about". Not only did our sales explode from this show, but we set sail to exhibit at other legal and court trade shows across the United States with similar results.

––––––

Final comment:

Imagine/See It, Feel It, Take Immediate Action. The vision formula is a tried-and-true process and is literally as old as time itself. If you look at every successful person in the world and could reverse engineer what they did to get to where they are, you'd be able to distill it down to the above formula. It's that easy, so try it. You'll see manifesting results in alignment with your vision.

SEVEN

SURROUND YOURSELF WITH THOSE
WHO WILL SUPPORT YOUR VISION

A braham Lincoln said, *"Give me six hours to chop down a tree and I will spend the first four sharpening the ax."* When you set out to achieve something, it's important to have the tools that you'll need, and one of those tools is the people you associate with and are surrounded by.

> *"...the people you habitually associate with determine as much as 95 percent of your success or failure in life."*

The people who influenced you in your formative years and the people you surround yourself with today may be the biggest influence on your behavior, attitudes and results. Take stock of the people you have attracted into your life and examine where they "come from" in consciousness. For example, do they come from a "growth" mindset, or conversely, do they live in a "victim" mindset, etc.? Who you hang out with speaks volumes about your secret "familiar" inheritance and about your desire to grow.

In the words of motivational speaker Jim Rohn, *"You are the average of the five people you spend the most time with."* The people you spend the most time with can significantly influence who you are. They determine what conversations dominate your attention. They affect which attitudes and behaviors you are regularly exposed to. Eventually you start to think like they think and behave like they behave. In fact, Dr. David McClelland of Harvard University writes, **"the people you habitually associate with determine as much as 95 percent of your success or failure in life."** That's huge and it has important consequences. Many times, the goal or dream we have will be bigger than our environment. It was for me at the age of twenty-two, and only when I broke free was I able to truly grow.

It's a fact of life, and most of you reading this can attest that some people hold us back, while others propel us forward. Some of you might be saying, "That's just the way it is, so you might as well accept it and learn how to deal with it instead of wishing reality was different." While that may be pragmatic, it can be a very limiting thought. You can't just hang out with negative people and expect to have a positive life. More importantly, if you do all the right things, but don't spend time with people who hold you to a higher standard, then you increase your chance of failure.

What I'm saying, with passion, is that when you decide to make a shift in your life, to have a goal, fulfill a dream, you may need to reconstruct your social environment. Don't let it depend on chance or on how it has always been, but consciously plan which opinions, attitudes and life philosophies you do and do not allow to be in your life. Not only can these people provide motivation, support, and counsel but also much-needed love, especially in times of strife or trouble. Picking people to surround yourself with can be difficult, but what can be even harder is letting those go who do not support your vision, especially if they're family.

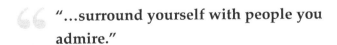

"...surround yourself with people you admire."

Family is very important to me, and in my latter years I can say that I'm truly blessed with the men and women whom I call family, i.e., Jeri, my children, and grandchildren, nieces, nephews, etc. While I've been there for them, they in turn have been there for me and each other. An interesting fact is that every one of them has invested in personal growth and shows up empowered, taking full responsibility for their lives and their choices.

IN CONCLUSION

Who you surround yourself with is not just important, it's critical. They will be there for a variety of reasons, one of them being to support your vision. So choose wisely. That said, I would like to propose one guiding principle you can use in deciding, and that is to *surround yourself with people you admire.*

We become like the people we (choose to) expose ourselves to. It follows that you can accelerate your personal growth in whatever direction you desire by spending time with people who *already are* who you want to *become.* That will infect you with the behaviors and attitudes that helped them achieve their success, making it more likely you will realize similar results in *your* life. So ask yourself these questions:

- Who do you spend the most time with?
- Who are the people you most admire?
- Are those two groups of people the same?

- Do they support your goals, visions?

And one final thing, it is a gift to have people in your life who challenge you with constructive criticism and probing questions, not in an effort to derail you but to understand your vision and challenge all its aspects.

EIGHT
WHY AM I IN THE PRESENCE OF...?

You've already read about this in previous chapters. It's so powerful I had to give it its own chapter so I could break it down.

I cannot tell you how many times, when events happened in my life, I found gold in asking myself *"Why am I in the presence of this event or situation?"* As I became aware that everything in the universe is "connected", it made more sense to become disciplined in asking this question on a regular basis. What I found was that when I asked the question, the true meaning of the event or situation was unveiled before me. I want to share a story with you that so vividly expresses the importance of including this question in your life.

————

RAY'S STORY

> *"It starts with understanding that everything is connected and there is purpose in every moment, including now,"*

In 2009, Jeri and I moved into a small gated community where most of the residents were from seventy to ninety years old. Being in our sixties, we were the kids on the block. As we met the locals, we were enthralled. They were wonderful people with diverse backgrounds living their senior years. In particular was an eighty-year-old neighbor named Ray, a retired CEO. His mind was as sharp as any thirty-to-forty-year-old "youngster". Ray was a widower who had lost his wife of fifty years a year earlier. He had this sweet dog name Conner, which he religiously walked every day. I would watch him as he and Conner passed by our condo. I couldn't help noticing the slow gait and slumped demeanor. Ray had confided in me that he was lost without his wife and was very unhappy; he wondered why he was still here. In essence, without his wife, he had lost his purpose.

On a particular day, I had an important meeting to attend at the office at 8:30 a.m., so I scheduled my departure time accordingly. I descended the steps from my condo, with my mind focused on preparing for the upcoming meeting. As I reached the bottom of the stairs,

Ray was walking by with Conner and I said hello. Ray returned the hello then stopped and turned towards me and asked, "Hey, Rod, you got a moment?" Automatically, my mind's thought was to respond with "I'm sorry, Ray, I've got to get to a meeting". However, my spiritual training kicked in; I took a breath and quietly asked myself, "Why am I in the presence of Ray at this moment?" With that, I surrendered to the moment and asked Ray what he wanted to talk to me about.

Ray told me again about how lonely and unhappy he had been since his wife's death. It was easy to feel his pain; as he expressed it in both his words and demeanor.

Then, out of nowhere, he told me how he had noticed I seemed happy all the time, and he wanted to know what my secret was. *"Oh, Ray, it's rather simple. It starts with understanding that everything is connected and there is purpose in every moment, including now,"* I said.

We chatted back and forth about what that meant, and then he asked me another question. "How do you make yourself happy when, as you know, I lost the love of my life a year ago?" I responded that it has to do with a simple daily exercise that I do without fail.

The exercise boils down to these four fundamental questions:

1. **What am I grateful for?**
2. **Who do I choose to be today?**

3. Who do I choose to be today when I
   forget #2?
4. What does Jeri need from me? (In Ray's case
   Mary.)

I then proceeded to speak about each question.

What am I grateful for?

I said, "Ray, when you wake up, don't just get up and
go about your day, think about what you are grateful for.
For example, you might be grateful that you opened
your eyes and are still here in life. You might take a deep
breath and be in gratitude for that breath and the next
breath and the next. In essence, be present with the abun-
dancy of the air that the universe provides and be
grateful for it.

"Sometimes you might get stuck and can't think
about something to be grateful about. If that happens,
look around your room and find an object to focus on.
For example, you might see a ballpoint pen on your
nightstand. Pick it up and think about the millions of
thoughts you are in the presence of that caused this
wonderful writing instrument to be on your nightstand.
The plastic came from plants that lived millions of years
ago and transformed into oil. Think about the life of the
plants and all the animals that ate them and became part

of its cellular journey. Think about the person, millions of years later, who noticed black ooze coming out of the ground and who started their journey of thoughts about what could become of this black ooze. Think about the chemists who figured out how to transform this oil into plastic; then think about the person who discovered ink and figured out a way to get it into a writing vessel; then think about the person who thought about how to combine the plastic carrier with the ink-delivery device. Think about the manufacturing and tooling that created the pen, and the people on the production line who made it happen. Then think about the shipping and marketing that caused the pen to be in the store you bought it from and so on and so on."

Ray just stood there in wonderment and told me he had never even considered what it took for that pen to be on his nightstand and how incredibly useful the pen was, as he took it for granted.

Who do I choose to be today?

I said to him, "Ray, after spending some moments on being grateful, now ask, who do I choose to be today? Most of us wake up and—depending on our sleep, dreams, our body chemistry and thoughts of what is in front of us today—almost robotically experience a mood or early theme for our day. Imagine if you could choose who you will be today. Yes, Ray, you can. For example, you could choose to be happy, and if you find your inner voice saying no you aren't, then choose to override it and choose to be happy. You might choose to be focused on being happy if that is what you see is needed. Your 'beingness' (state of mind) is an inner choice not the result of outer factors."

Who do I choose to be today when I forgot what I chose earlier?

"Ray, it is normal for the mind to wander throughout the day and cause you to forget what you chose earlier about your beingness. We depend on our SubConscious Mind to run our lives each day, and it sometimes forgets who is in charge. For example, it's 11:30 a.m. and after declaring at 8:30 a.m. that you choose to be happy today, something reminds you of Mary not being here and you feel sad. Notice it and then choose again to be happy. This is not a test and you are not wrong for forgetting to follow your word about being happy. Just choose again and keep choosing again and again throughout your day. After a while, your mind gets the message that you are the commander of your mind and not the other way around."

What does Mary need from me today?

As soon as I uttered these words, Ray asked me how this could be, because Mary was no longer here. I responded, "Ray, she actually is here. She is here in your heart and soul and in all the things around you that were present in her life. Most importantly, she is inside you and lives within you all the time." When I said these words, he reached out with tears in his eyes, hugged me and thanked me for taking the time to be with him.

Interestingly, when I started this moment with Ray, I was concerned I would be late for my meeting. What's funny is I actually arrived on time. I surrendered to my question of "Why am I in the presence of?" and it all worked out. I got to give someone, a soul hurting from loss, some actionable advice, and I still arrived on time to my meeting without missing a beat.

I didn't see Ray for a few months; then one day, I came out on my deck and saw Ray walking briskly with Conner, head up and light of foot. I went down to chat and met a Ray I had not seen before. He was excited and animated as he told me what that moment a few months ago meant to him. He told me about sitting down with a pen in his hand and being mesmerized, realizing the millions of thoughts he was holding in his hand, and being humbled by the experience. He told me how he asked what Mary needed from him each day, and that his inner Mary commanded him to be happy and find his purpose again.

We moved away from that community, and I later found out that Mary must have told him he needed to be married, because he found a wonderful companion and married her.

————

ASK THE QUESTION

Asking *"Why am I in the presence of...?"* is a powerful question to add to your inner conversation with yourself anytime something arises. As I trust you know by now, your SubConscious Mind wants to keep things in a certain order developed over the years of learning your habits and thoughts. It will, oftentimes, automatically drive your decisions in a "familiar" direction and cause you to miss some incredible moments, such as my meeting with Ray. Imagine how he felt and then imagine how I felt in facilitating Ray's choosing a different perspective about life. Now it's your turn! Use this question as a way to enrich your life and share it with others. I promise you, the "now" and "wow" moments in your life will become very different than what you thought they would be.

NINE
EVERYTHING HAPPENS WITHIN YOU

When I became the Dean of Boys at Thomas Jefferson High School, I changed my graduate school focus from Marketing to an MBA in counseling. One course required us to create an outreach program focused on personal growth. My group consisted of boy students from Thomas Jefferson High School. Around the fourth meeting, a student's mother approached me and said she was impressed by how her son was taking to my program, and she was interested in putting together a "consciousness raising" group with her girlfriends. I went to my professor and asked if she had a woman in mind who could lead the group. To my surprise, she challenged me to lead the group, which I was apprehensive to do, given I was a male.

I met with the group of six women every two weeks. Everyone in the group was a single mom receiving little or no child support. Most of the children were out of wedlock, and only two of the fathers stayed involved with the kids.

In my first two meetings, I was a fish out of water. After the second meeting, I decided to reach out to my spiritual connection for support. Before closing my eyes to sleep, I asked the Universe to send me something I could use to break through with these women and create something meaningful. The next morning, I woke up about 5:00 a.m. with thoughts swirling in my head about a challenging process to offer the women. In our next meeting, I introduced them to this process. (I would encourage you to actually experience this process with yourself.)

Below is the exercise I gave to them and what happened:

- "Close your eyes."
- "Think about someone who makes your skin crawl; someone who causes a strong negative reaction in you; someone who you can't help but be in judgment about; someone you wish didn't have such power over you by the emotional reaction they cause in you. Raise your hand when you have someone in mind."
- Only two hands went up, so I told them I would help them with a hint:

- "This person has a name (long pause) and their name is (long pause) asshole." (Pause.) I continued, "Some of you might be uncomfortable with saying this word, however, you know what it stands for."
- Giggles went through the room as all hands were now raised. I continued:
- "I want you to imagine that you have died, passed through and are now sitting with God, whoever God is for you. You realize you are in this evolved space with God; however, sitting next to God is 'the asshole'. You are confused about why this asshole is in your heaven. So you ask God why he/she is here?"
- "God warmly leans forward and softly whispers, '**This was your teacher**. I, God, sent this teacher to you so you could learn about yourself.'"
- "God continues: 'I have a very important question to ask you. How did you do with your teacher when you were on earth and had the opportunity to grow; what did you learn; how would you measure your success in learning from your teacher?'"
- I then went silent to have them process what they had just experienced.

- "When you are ready, open your eyes and come back to the present."

The women then shared about their "teacher" and what this process was like for them. I encouraged them to think hard about this teacher and let us know when we reconvened anything they learned.

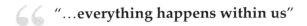 "...**everything happens within us**"

At the beginning of the next session one of the women, I'll call her "Lydia", came in with very high energy and told us she had something to share about an experience she had with her teacher. (We found it powerful to substitute the word "teacher" for the "ass-hole" word.) Lydia went on to describe how her ex-husband (her teacher) did participate time wise (how-ever, no child support) with the kids by picking them up every other Saturday and returning them Sunday after-noon. She told us how, upon his arrival, she would herd the kids to the door and give him instructions about food and cleanliness and getting them back on time.

Lydia had never invited him in, so on this last week-end, she decided to take a different approach. She left the kids in their room and went to the door to invite him in. He hesitated, then followed her into the apartment. She offered him some coffee and asked how he was doing and was he happy; how was his mother doing, etc., etc. *She stayed away from anything to do with money.* He loosened up and they spoke for about thirty minutes. Lydia told us how she realized she was the one getting in the way of having a healthy relationship with her kids' father.

Some of the women had tears in their eyes and gave her big hugs and congratulated her. Others in the group shared some of their insights. We spent the remaining time listening to each other's breakthroughs. They didn't want to leave because the energy was so high.

Well, at the beginning of our next session, Lydia came bursting into the meeting a few minutes late, fumbling through her purse (known as "pocketbooks" in New York, which I never quite grasped). She pulled out a check for $2,000 that her "teacher" had given her that morning. She told us how he had apologized for not keeping his end of the financial bargain of being responsible for the kids.

After all the whooping and hollering settled down, we discussed the concept of how "**everything happens within us**" and that external factors, circumstances and people trigger what is already inside us planted by prior life experiences. I call this the simple principle of "**Resonation**". *If something is not already inside your mind or psyche, it will not resonate, and you will have* *no reaction. If you have a reaction, it is not the person's (or circumstances') issue but rather your own. At that moment, if you are truly owning your life, you will look within to uncover what the source of your reaction is.* It is important to note that this works both ways. In other words, when you see and experience someone or something that moves you, it is because that quality or value is already in you.

Let's use an example. You and your husband/wife are at dinner with some Japanese acquaintances and you just expressed a strong opinion on a political matter. One of your Japanese acquaintances looks you in the eye and says, *"Anata ga orokana bakadearu."* You have no reaction to what was just said because you don't speak Japanese and it doesn't resonate.

Now imagine you are at the same dinner with English-speaking acquaintances and one of them tells you, "You are a stupid idiot" (translation of *Anata ga orokana bakadearu"*). Chances are you might react because the concept and feelings of being called a stupid idiot are well established in your psyche. Let's take it one step further. Think about how you would react if at the same dinner after making your opinion known, your English-speaking acquaintance called you an "asshole". It's not a far stretch to think you might react.

The truth is that you wouldn't resonate and react to being called an asshole if the feeling of being an asshole didn't already reside within. All that this person did was stimulate a thought within. That person did not put that pre-existing thought in, and again, if you truly own your life, you would not blame them and subsequently you would not react. **An alternative responsible reaction would be to ask the person why they think you are an asshole and take the feedback "within" for a reality check.**

This asshole process is very effective with groups and individuals if those people are in a space of being willing to look within for their answers. So many people I have done this process with tell me about the wonderful breakthroughs they have had using this simple tool. It is as simple as noticing, for example, the dialogue in your head when someone cuts you off on the freeway. Everything is happening within you based upon internal beliefs, typically as a victim. The mind loves victimhood because you get to be "right". In that state, it doesn't want you to imagine or know that there may be an emergency and a husband is rushing to the hospital because his wife is in labor as he cut you off. As an alternative, just say "thank you" to your teacher.

———

VICTIM CONSCIOUSNESS

The victim consciousness that lives within each of us loves to drift back and forth, scanning the space for reasons to be right. In fact, most relationships are burdened because of this need to be "right". Truthfully ask yourself how many times an argument between you and your spouse, significant other, child, friend, or extended family had to do with both sides trying to be right no matter what the topic is? I will bet you, if you're honest, that the answer is about one hundred percent.

Here's an exercise that illustrates the point:

- There's a little old lady with a cane standing at a curb. This gangster-looking thug forcefully knocks her to the ground and she's rolling in pain. The crowd around her reacts and starts yelling at the thug, telling him what a bad person he is. They speak to her and tell her she should press charges.

- The lady sits up and tells the crowd to stop yelling at him because he saved her life. She said she was about to enter the crosswalk and a taxi would have hit her if she had done so, and that she was so grateful to him for knocking her down. The crowd, now understanding what had really happened, realizes his intentions and starts apologizing to the thug.

- The thug responds to the crowd by saying he didn't try to save her life but just wanted to knock her down and steal her purse. The crowd, now with this new information, returns to making him wrong and letting him know what an evil person he is.
- The crowd then explains to the lady what he had said about wanting to knock her down and again suggests she should press charges.
- The lady repeats what she had told them earlier about how he saved her life and therefore she does not care about his intentions because she is alive today because of him. She goes on to say that there are blessings in everything when you see the entire picture and to consider that our victim consciousness and righteous mind is locked and loaded "looking for bear" regardless of the truth.

———

SUBWAY STORY
(Looking from a different perspective)

I grew up in New York City, and riding the subway was common. There's a story about a man riding with his kids on the subway. The kids were young and running up and down the aisle and being very loud, disturbing some passengers. The father just sat there ignoring the kids and seemingly oblivious to the annoyance some passengers were experiencing.

Finally, one woman had had enough and spoke to the father. "What's wrong with you? Your kids are loud and disturbing other passengers, including me." The woman felt so "right" about her point to him. The father turns to the woman and says, "I'm sorry, the kids and I are coming home from the funeral service after burying my wife, who just died of cancer. I felt I needed them to blow off some steam. Again, I'm sorry." The woman was at a consciousness crossroads. She could either continue in her righteousness (aka "victim consciousness") and make him wrong, regardless of the facts, or shift her consciousness to one of empathy. In this case, the woman embraced the facts and comforted the man.

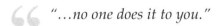 *"…no one does it to you."*

The above story could be placed anywhere and under many different circumstances. It's all about perspective and shifting away from the mindset that you've been victimized to one of empathy. Growth is a choice and sometimes requires focused work. Sometimes it seems so hard to take the higher/inner ground; however, if you want to grow, it's essential you do so. By the way, in this process of growth, "suffering is optional", meaning it's a choice. And remember, *everything happens within you and no one does it to you*. It is important to reflect on how your reactions to life experiences are typically driven by the programs inside you.

Whether you're dealing with the "asshole" in your life or the need to be "right", you are making a choice. What I'm saying is that things can be different, and the answers to the questions you have can always be found within you. Call it what you want, God, Universe, etc.; the answers or solutions to the most difficult questions or problems reside inside one place... *YOU*.

TEN
LIFE LESSONS

T ake a moment and reflect on the times you were in total *reaction* to a person or circumstance. In the stories I shared in the previous chapter, you can see how taking a different perspective along with taking full responsibility for yourself can result in a much more positive outcome. Notice that all the feeling was going on in your body, not someone else's. Nelson Mandela once said, *"Resentment is like drinking poison and then hoping it will kill your enemies."*

 "Resentment is like drinking poison and then hoping it will kill your enemies."

Look back into your life experiences, with a new sense of

adventure, and be open to discovering what worked, what didn't work, and *rewriting your story from a place of true ownership and responsibility.* See that whatever you were challenged with happened *"for you"* and *not "to you"*.

FAILURE

I know of multiple people who were fired from their job, thought it was unfair, and felt devastated. Interesting that out of that experience a whole new world opened up with a better job or, in some cases, even starting a new company. Therefore, I am not a fan of the word "failure". It's too black and white with negative connotations. Instead, *I think in a more fluid way about the challenges I face and their subsequent results.*

People have often asked me what my biggest failure was. Because failure doesn't fit into my success vocabulary, I find that hard to answer because I don't consider things that don't work out as failures but rather as the results of my well-intended actions. The results are neither good nor bad. They are the perfect effect that was created by my thoughts and actions. Some effects work and some effects don't work. The challenges that show up are also perfect in that they are exactly what is needed to go through to get to the next level. Each challenge is a growth opportunity. My wife, Jeri, often says, *"In our greatest challenges come our greatest gifts."* You just need to be open to them. We don't always see those gifts while we are in the midst of our challenges; however, trust that the gifts are there.

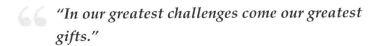

> *"In our greatest challenges come our greatest gifts."*

What I'm suggesting you do is redefine what failure is, or just don't use the word because you will now look at those times where "it didn't work out", or failures, as "results of my well-intended actions". It's a shift, but as Dr. Wayne Dyer said years ago, *"Change the way you look at things, and the things you look at change."*

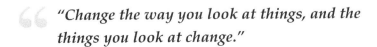

> *"Change the way you look at things, and the things you look at change."*

FEAR

Webster's Dictionary defines *fear* as:

noun
an unpleasant emotion caused by the belief that

someone or something is dangerous, likely to cause pain, or a threat.

But what is it really? You can't touch it; it doesn't exist in the confines of our three-dimensional world because it's all in our minds. I've often heard the phrase "fear of failure" in reference to what holds people back in their life. I've addressed failure above and will now focus on the concept (thought) of "fear".

Fear is nothing more than your inherited SubConscious Mind trying to keep things "familiar" and "safe". *The fear I am talking about is not one of violence but rather of "change".* Choosing to get married is change. Choosing a new job is change. Your SubConscious Mind does not like change because it views change as a threat to the status quo. Choose to *"welcome fear"*, for it is a great indicator that you are growing and changing. You can take the easy out and run from your fear; however, where has that gotten you in your life?

So, embrace your fear, challenge yourself, and choose to own your life like never before.

ELEVEN
THE JOURNEY NEVER ENDS

The lessons I've shared in the book have helped me considerably grow businesses, wealth, and enabled me to become a better man, father, husband and friend.

As of this book's publication, I find myself retired from the company I founded, which I sold in 2015; but I'm still very busy creating and growing. Whether that be opportunities like investing in start-up companies or mentoring those around me. I am grateful to be surrounded by my family, with whom I find great joy and purpose. My children have all grown and have become, in their own right, successful and thriving.

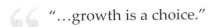 "...growth is a choice."

If you've made it this far in the book, you have experienced a journey, my journey of self-discovery. But like I said at the beginning of the book, what I've been able to accomplish is possible for you to do. I was a C student, did well in sports, but when it came to knowing that I had more to give, I was lost; so much that in order to turn my life around, I needed a reboot of sorts. This reboot shifted my thinking and how I interact with the world on a daily basis. I now have a healthy money consciousness, I challenged and overcame many of the limited beliefs that were poured into me, I aligned my beliefs with my vision, I surrounded myself with people who support my vision, and I know that everything happens within me. I have effectively used these tools and new ways of thinking to propel me to success in all areas of my life, and I fervently continue to ask, **"why am I in the presence of…?"** to create more opportunities for growth.

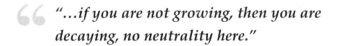
> *"…if you are not growing, then you are decaying, no neutrality here."*

Remember, *the lessons in this book are something you practice every day*. This isn't a crash diet in life, this is about making **big shifts, in small bites**, that will have to be tended to daily. Your journey of self-discovery and improvement never ends; it is ongoing. As I've mentioned before, *growth is a choice* and, in my experience, the most powerful one anyone can make. It is in our growth that our life's vision takes traction. I believe that *if you are not growing, then you are decaying, no neutrality here.* Breathe that into your soul and choose growth, over and over again, and watch your life blossom in alignment with your vision. *Your inner challenge will always be your inherited beliefs fighting like mad to preserve the status quo.* Stand tall on your choice to grow and remind your MIND who is in charge, and when you do, you'll be able to take possession of your secret inheritance...*the authentic YOU.*

———

One Final thought

What I have shared with you can be life changing. I encourage you to take immediate action:

- Think about key elements in the book that resonated, write them down and meditate on them regularly.
- Go back and look at the highlighted thoughts and reflect on each one and how it relates to

you. *Notice any resistance to those thoughts and ponder where the resistance is coming from and if the resistance is in alignment with your vision or dragging it down.*

- Use the questionnaire in the back of this book to discover the source of some of your attitudes about money. Choose your own beliefs about money.
- Bless people who have money.
- Be grateful when paying bills (value for value).
- Do the Price Tag Challenge in the back of this book to experience your internal thoughts about money.
- Be *"willing"* to have what you say you want, even when you don't see a clear path.
- Retrain your mind by integrating the "**Recall**" exercise, in the back of this book, regularly into your life.
- Create a vision for your life. **See it, feel it, take immediate action**.
- Always ask, **"Why am I in the presence of...?"** and let the answer unfold.
- Use the asshole exercise as a reminder to thank your *"teacher"* next time one appears.
- Focus on what you discovered by reading my journey and reset your life accordingly.

- Be ferocious about your growth and authenticity.

And remember, this is the *fun stuff.*

TOOLS, STORIES AND INSIGHTS FROM MY JOURNEY

TWELVE

WALZ SECRET INHERITANCE QUESTIONNAIRE

Walz Secret Inheritance Questionnaire

READ CAREFULLY

L ike I said before in the story about purchasing Blake for Jeri, your journey of tackling your limited beliefs and expanding your money consciousness is something you'll have to do daily; however, there has to be a baseline, a starting point. **Do you know your beliefs about money?** Can you trace back to when you first developed them or they were poured into you? I mentioned the importance of going back into your life and sourcing the beginnings of your inner beliefs so you can understand better why you show up and believe the way you do. As a gift, I'd like to share with you a questionnaire that I developed with Jeri and used in seminars and with friends. This will help you set a baseline and give you a deeper understanding.

Questionnaire Purpose

Money is like oxygen in our life, so it's imperative that we understand our consciousness about it. A simple question *"What do you believe about money?"* is a good start. What if it's true that you create and attract results at the level of your consciousness? If so, it might be worthwhile to examine the thoughts about money you secretly inherited from your early life to see what is in your soil affecting your economic results.

This exercise can be very enlightening and fun if you *"choose in"* and purposefully take yourself on. Your answers hold a key to understanding your inherited beliefs about money, beliefs that will influence almost everything you do in your career and personal life. These beliefs were poured into you, just as your first language was poured into you, *without any filter or any vote*. They are neither right/wrong nor good/bad. They are just what values others had, in your formative years, in shaping your consciousness. As you become aware of what got poured in, you are then better equipped to reshape your beliefs in alignment with your vision for your life. We trust you will be stimulated to do so and grow from this experience.

. . .

Instructions

This questionnaire focuses on you, your dad and your mom. If you were not raised by one or either of them, then use the people who were around you most in years 0–12*. It is best to go quietly inside your mind and visualize being back in your childhood home as a *little boy* or *little girl*. Answer these questions **intuitively** *with the first thing that comes to your mind*. When you get the answer, stay there for a moment and notice any feelings that might have been triggered, then write down the answer. Remember, these are the thoughts and beliefs that got poured into your subconscious mind with no filtering and will provide you with insights as to the foundation for your beliefs. **If you are not sure, for example, what your mother or father thought in the context of one of these questions, just answer the best you can as to** *what you think they would have said or believed.* The most important thing here is to be spontaneous with your answers and have fun on this journey home!

- **If you see an asterisk (*), then answer relating to when you were 0–12 years old. This is very important to get the most value.**
- **Remember: write down your first thought.**

Write your answers down and review each and see what memories come up. Also, feel free to share the questionnaire with significant others (parents, adult children, spouses, etc.) then discuss what you discovered. It can enlighten and open up healthy dialogue. You might just better appreciate and understand each other.

IMPORTANT: most of the questions have an asterisk (*), which means you answer the questions from your little-boy or little-girl memories prior to 12 years old.

You

1. What do you believe about money?

2. What is your earliest memory of money?*

3. What is your first memory of your *making* money?* What were you doing? How much did you earn?

. . .

4. What were you feeling about making this money in #3?*

5. What did you do with the money in #3?* How did you feel?*

6. Complete this sentence: Rich people are…

7. Complete this sentence: Money is…

8. Did you consider yourself poor, middle-class or rich?*

Dad

1. What did your dad do for a living?* Was he salaried or commissioned?*

2. How much money does/did he approximately average per year?*

• • •

3. What did your dad say about money?* (If he never said anything, what do you think he would say?)

4. What did your dad say about people with money?* (If he never said anything, what do you think he would say?)

5. Did your dad consider himself poor, middle-class or rich?*

6. What was the riskiest thing your dad did with money?
*

7. When you asked your dad for money, how did he respond?* How did you feel?*

8. What is a key memory of your dad choosing to spend money on you?* What was the money for?* How much was it?* How did it make you feel?*

9. How much cash did your dad carry on him?*

• • •

10. How much cash in his pocket would have made your dad uncomfortable?* Why?*

11. Did your dad ever buy something special for himself? * If yes, what?*

Mom

1. What did your mom do for a living?* Was she salaried or commissioned?*

2. How much money does/did she approximately average per year?*

3. What did your mom say about money?* (If she never said anything, what do you think she would say?)

4. What did your mom say about people with money?* (If she never said anything, what do you think she would say?)

...

5. Did your mom consider herself poor, middle-class or rich?*

6. What was the riskiest thing your mom did with money?*

7. When you asked your mom for money, how did she respond?* How did you feel?*

8. What is a key memory of your mom choosing to spend money on you?* What was the money for?* How much was it?* How did it make you feel?*

9. How much cash did your mom carry on her?*

10. How much cash in her pocket would have made your mom uncomfortable?* Why?*

11. Did your mom ever buy something special for herself?* If yes, what?*

...

Mom and Dad

1. Who controlled the money in your household, and who was the breadwinner?*

2. Did your mom and dad argue over money?* If yes, what about?*

You Again

1. What's a lot of money?

2. Complete this sentence: A rich person makes more than $_per year.

3. How much cash do you typically carry each day?

4. How much cash in your pocket or purse would make you feel uncomfortable? Why?

• • •

5. What is the most amount of cash that you have ever had in your personal possession? $_How did you feel?

6. Complete this sentence: I will be well off when I am making a minimum of $_per year?

7. Who is the richest person you know <u>personally</u>?

8. What is your belief about rich people? "They are..."

9. If you made a lot of money, what would change in your life?

10. If you had an idea for a business or product, who would you bounce the idea off of and why?

11. Regarding #10, who wouldn't you bounce it off of and why?

. . .

12. Recall something in your life that you had a clear vision about having and you got it. What was it and how did you feel when you got it?

––––––––

Retraining Your Mind to Shift Your Beingness (Recall Exercise)

"How are you?" We are asked that question so many times as in "Good morning, how are you?" Often our answer only touches the surface and we respond, "I'm fine, how are you?" A more probing question is "How are you doing?" In answering that question, we tend to dig deeper and see what our feelings are emotionally, physically, and spiritually. In essence, this is what we call *"beingness"* or, for some, "energy or attitude". We have been trained to just accept the way we feel, as though we have no control over it. You actually have the power to shift your beingness, in a moment.

What I'm about to share with you was a critical tool for me rebooting my life. The basic premise of this exercise is that the Subconscious Mind is used to automatically being in control. This exercise changes the course and puts you more in control of what the Subconscious Mind presents to you.

Instructions: You will ask your mind to recall something. Whatever it sends up from memory, just say *"thank you"*. It's okay if the thought the mind sends up does not make sense. Different than the previous questionnaire, *it is important not to dwell on what got sent up.* The purpose of this exercise is to train your mind to listen to your requests and respond accordingly rather than the mind being in control of what it sends up. It has nothing to do with the content of the thought but rather about "you" being in control. In time, you will be able to command your mind to send up what you request.

Here's an example:

- Recall a time when I got physically hurt. (Mind) Memory of falling at six years old. (You) Thank you.
- Recall a time when I laughed at something funny. (Mind) Memory of my mom crying. (You) Thank you.
- Recall a time when I won at something. (Mind) Fifth grade and a bad report card to show my parents. (You) Thank you.
- Etc., etc. Be as creative as you can with your questions.

During this process, it is easy to get distracted by the thought that the mind sends up from memory. If you dwell on the thought, *you get the booby prize, for it is your Subconscious Mind trying to be in control again.*

Stop dwelling and return to the exercise. I spent a year of my life regularly doing this exercise. It's so easy to do, anytime. The more I did the exercise, the more I was able to control my beingness on command. For example, if I wasn't feeling confident, I would instruct my mind to remember how it felt to feel confident and choose to be confident.

By the way, this exercise can be a lot of fun noticing how the SubConscious Mind tries to get you off track focusing on the content of each thought that the mind sends up. *It also confirms that you have an inner voice that is quite potent.* In any case, grow well with it.

THIRTEEN

STORIES FROM MY JOURNEY

A s I was writing this book, I had so many stories to tell, some of which you'll read below. They didn't fit nicely into the lessons I was conveying in the preceding chapters, but each one that follows illustrates tools or tricks that have helped me become a successful entrepreneur, businessman, father, husband and friend.

―――――

DAY GLOW GOLF BALLS

As much as I had been a mediocre C student in high school and college, that all changed when I went to grad school. I started out on a path to an MBA focused on Marketing. The courses were typically taught by businesspeople who brought real-life business into the classroom. My interest level was high and my grades always between A's and B's. In one of the courses, each of us was challenged to come up with a new product and provide a paper and presentation on our ideas.

What was interesting back then, in the early seventies, was that most of the research you did was at the New York Public Library, in Manhattan, because it housed a huge database of information on microfiche media. If you needed something, you went to an index file on the topic and put in a request to have the roll of microfiche pulled. You would load it in a viewing machine and start scrolling through until you found what you wanted. You would then take copious notes by hand, repeating what you had seen. In writing your paper, we would use a portable typewriter with "white out" strips for correcting typos. This was quite tedious, so you did most of your editing on your handwritten notepad.

My idea was based on a real-life experience of looking for my golf balls in the rough. I thought if the balls were brightly colored, they would be easier to find. I was so excited to present my paper on "Day Glow Golf Balls". Well, I got a B- with a commentary from the professor that stated I didn't consider enough the resistance of the golf community because the balls were traditionally white. My professor was running an advertising agency as his day job, so I gracefully accepted the grade and the comments.

Roll forward a few years and I'm on a golf course when an errant shot, from another fairway, comes my way. There it was, a bright yellow Wilson golf ball. I was so excited that I got in touch with my old professor. We both laughed; however, *he encouraged me to never let anyone or their opinion (even his) stand in the way of new ideas.*

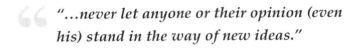

> *"...never let anyone or their opinion (even his) stand in the way of new ideas."*

Upon further research, as an aside, I found that in 1923 Wilson Sporting Goods introduced Canary Yellow and Oriole Orange golf balls. One of the big reasons they didn't catch on was because of their high price of $10.75 a dozen, which would be equivalent to $136.00 today. They reintroduced them in 1982 and garnered 20% of the market. Lesson learned!

———

CAN I HAVE THAT BUSINESS CARD BACK?

In 1975, I owned a Victor calculator dealership selling electronic and programmable calculators in San Diego's north county. I hired a new salesman named Michael, who had just gotten back from Vietnam as a medic. He had no sales experience; however, I decided to work with him and, after some training, took him out cold-calling on businesses in our territory.

We entered a small law office, and he nervously asked the receptionist if they were in the market for a calculator. She took his card and went into the attorney's office to inquire. Fortunately, she left the door ajar about eight inches, where I was able to observe her conversation with the attorney. *I watched as the attorney tore up the business card and threw it in the wastebasket.* The receptionist came back to us and informed us that they had no need now but would keep the card and contact us if something came up in the future.

Michael thanked her and started for the door. I, however, turned to the receptionist and explained to her that Michael was brand new and we had only made him a small supply of business cards, as he was in training. *"I know from experience you are probably not interested, and it would mean a lot to me if you could return Michael's business card to him."* She stood there frozen, then said she would be right back. She went into the attorney's office, this time closing the door completely. I can only imagine the conversation. A few minutes later, the door opened, and she told us that an appointment had cancelled, and he could spend a few minutes with him now.

Once together, I started by asking questions about his law practice. He mentioned his specialty was real estate and real estate investing. I asked what type of investing and he mentioned primarily apartment complexes. I asked him if he had to do Internal Rate of Return (IRR) calculations. He said yes. In those years, if you invested in an apartment complex, you could show any losses against your personal tax returns; therefore, investing in them was popular. IRR calculations were an essential tool to determine projected profits or losses over a span of years. I asked the attorney to give me an overview of how he did those calculations today. He did and it was quite tedious and long.

That year, Victor had introduced a new programmable calculator. It had no display and limited alphanumeric output on the tape. At the time, it was breakthrough technology. One of the programs written for it was IRR calculations. I told the attorney what we had, then went to my car and brought in the programmable calculator. I then had him enter real data, which took about two minutes, and out came a printed tape displaying the results over the next five years. He was in shock because he then went on to tell me how it would take a few hours to do the same calculation. Well, he bought two of those calculators that day, all because he was "embarrassed" by tearing up a business card. *Michael learned an important lesson about being present and observant (conscious), at all times, in the sales process.*

———

YOU NEVER ASKED TO VALIDATE YOUR PARKING

As I mentioned earlier, I owned a foreclosure software company whose main product produced all the documents necessary for a California foreclosure trustee. It also produced the automated WALZ Certified Mail forms, which I later patented. When I first entered the trustee world, I had no competition, but that eventually changed. Now, I was one of three companies presenting our solutions to a mortgage company/trustee in West Hollywood. I finally got a call from the owner indicating he wanted to go with my solution, and he asked if I could bring the contract to a lunch venue the next day.

As we sat down, I asked him why he went with us, *since we were $10,000 higher in price.* He smiled and said that all the systems pretty much did the same thing; however, of the three companies presenting their solution, *I was the only one who did not ask him to validate the parking fee in the building.* He went on to say that as much as the validation fee was a drop in the bucket, he recognized that I respected his bottom line by not asking him to pay and that he felt secure that I would be there for him going forward.

This is such a valuable lesson in scarcity consciousness. The other companies were focused on their own nickels and dimes and missing the big picture. My not asking to have my parking validated (paid for) showed the client respect, which he picked up on. *Always make it about the client first.*

 "Always make it about the client first."

I SEEDED THE FORMS

If you've never had a US patent, you may not appreciate that while owning a patent does protect you, it costs a lot to defend it. Many times, start-ups just don't have that defense fund sitting around.

When Jeri and I got our first patent on the Walz Certified Mailer in 1987, we found out there was such a thing as patent insurance. Understanding the cost of defense, we quickly bought it, even though it was quite pricey. In our first year selling the WALZ Certified Mailers nationally, we encountered ten companies who blatantly copied our forms and stopped ordering from us. Thank the Universe we had the insurance because, with it, this start-up company had the financial clout to overcome the patent infringers. I'd like to share with you one of the more poignant stories.

A very large automobile manufacturer had a finance division that was ordering 25,000 WALZ Certified Mailers per month for their delinquent borrowers. After doing business together for over two years, they went quiet and stopped ordering. I tried and tried to speak with them, and no one would return my calls.

I, as always, had developed a close telephone relationship with the manager of the print/mail department who used our forms. Their operations were in Texas, so I flew out, unannounced, to stop by and meet with her. She was so excited to finally meet me in person, and I quickly realized she knew nothing of the gravity of the situation. She told me they had to switch suppliers because they had a companywide mandate to buy all forms from another company (ours were manufactured by Moore Business Forms). Before I left, I asked her if she could provide me with some samples of the other company's forms, and she did.

In my car I was quickly able to determine that the other forms company had exactly copied our form sets. Now, what no one knew was that in the design I had *"seeded"* the WALZ Certified Mailer form set with benign copy that looked like it made sense, yet it didn't. I will share with you, in a moment, why this was critical in resolving the issue with the client.

I placed a call to the client's legal department and was able to speak with the attorney who had overseen the patent issue when they changed manufacturers. First, I explained that not only did we have a patent, but I had $1,000,000 of patent insurance with a $10,000 deductible and they needed to square things up with me or I would turn it over to the insurance company. That got his attention to listen further. He made the point that the other company's legal department had assured them that their version did not infringe on ours. I asked him if he had a copy of both the WALZ Certified Mailer and the other company's form set, which he did.

For background, the WALZ Certified Mailer, at that time, was a four-part continuous form designed for dot matrix printers. Whatever you printed on the top went through to Parts 2, 3 and 4 using a chemical/carbon technology. This was before the age of laser printers, and it was imperative that you line up the starting point correctly so that all remaining data points got printed in their correct slots.

The WALZ Certified Mailer consisted of four parts. Part 1 was designed to be a cover sheet insert for a #10 window envelope to address the Certified Mail letter.

Part 2 was designed to be a cover sheet insert for a #10 window envelope to address the corresponding First-Class Mail letter (First-Class Mail was used to ensure the mail got delivered without the ability to refuse delivery). Part 3 was the USPS Certified white sheet with corresponding Certified Mail label attached on the right side. Part 4 was the green Return Receipt. On Part 1 (top sheet of the 4-part form), we placed the words "Line 1" to the left of the start line for the Name and address fields to assure correct printing of all fields in their allotted areas.

With the above in mind, I asked the attorney why we placed on Part 1 the words *"Line 1"*. He, with an attitude, said, "Mr. Walz, it's obvious that it is there to help align the form in the printer." I moved onto Part 2 and Part 3, neither of which contained the words "Line 1" because they served no purpose, being that the print operator couldn't see them when aligning the form. Then I moved the focus to Part 4, the Return Receipt. I asked the attorney to go through the form line by line. He immediately pointed out the words *"Line 1"*, and I asked him why those words were there. He told me he didn't know why those words were there because the print operator couldn't see them for alignment. My reply was, *"Well, I know why those words are there. I seeded the form with those innocuous words to capture companies who try to circumvent our patented design. The words have no other purpose."* There was a moment of silence followed by a soft-toned, "Rod, what do we need to do to resolve this?"

Knowing that he now knew we had the financial and factual clout to enter litigation, I let him know that we appreciated the long-term relationship and wanted to continue that relationship. I requested that he should immediately place an order for 25,000 forms and upon receipt cause their remaining inventory of the other company's forms to be destroyed with a confirmation letter to follow. They complied and remained a loyal client for years.

The importance of having protected intellectual property is invaluable. Being preemptively clever helps too.

TRAYS AND TRAYS OF CERTIFIED MAIL LEFT BEHIND

Because of our high success in automating Certified Mail nationally, I garnered a reputation as an expert regarding same. One day I got a phone call from a *New York Times* reporter who asked me if I was aware of the USPS holding back the delivery of Certified Mail being sent to the Illinois Department of Revenue in Springfield, IL, and a few other states. I told him that I wasn't aware, and he explained that he was investigating a rumor that large volumes of Certified Mail, with tax returns inside, were being held up at the post office in Springfield. We spoke a few more minutes, and knowing the catastrophic potential of this matter, I asked if I could call him back and hung up.

I immediately called the USPS vice president of the Great Lakes region, who I knew from his days in San Diego. I told his secretary, "You don't know me, but your boss does, and he needs to call me immediately." About ten minutes later the VP called me, wondering what could be so urgent. I explained the situation about the reporter and what he had said. I told him the reporter was awaiting my call. He said he would look into it and get back to me. About an hour later he called me back and explained what had happened.

At this time, the USPS was introducing barcodes that could be scanned onto Certified Mail. At the Springfield, IL, post office that received the Certified Mail for the state, the USPS clerk was required to scan the barcodes on each envelope, which in turn printed out a report for the state to sign for the trays of Certified Mail upon delivery. The clerk who was to do the scanning had not received the printer to print out the report and, unbeliev-ably, had held back trays and trays (a room full) of Certi-fied Mail because "I didn't have a printer". The effect of his actions was monumental. All those tax returns were now being delivered late, and penalties could be applied to each return.

The VP was astounded by the stupidity of the clerk and had a printer driven down to that clerk that day. He thanked me for the heads-up, and I told him I would mute the incident as best I could. I then called the *New York Times* reporter and explained that this was simply an issue of a clerk not thinking things through and not an endemic problem of the USPS. He appreciated my input and wrote a more tempered piece in the *Times* than he was originally set out to print.

———

"WE CAN'T GIVE YOU THE DATA, IT'S CONFIDENTIAL."

I originally created the Walz Item Tracking System (WITS), in 1990, to track FedEx, UPS and USPS accountable items on receiving docks *after* the items were signed for by the receiving clerk. Up until then, receiving docks had to manually verify the item counts from the carrier, sort the items by internal delivery, create a handwritten delivery manifest to collect signatures, and deliver the items. WITS automated the entire process, and entities like FedEx, USPS, HP and many more relied on it for their internal receipt and deliveries. At Compaq Computer in Houston, employing 30,000 employees, WITS was invaluable, and they included WITS instruction in their corporate operations' manual. What was funny is that they played off the name WALZ and made it into a verb and instructed everyone to *"WALTZ"* all internal delivery items.

There were many poignant stories of success pioneering an automated approach to an extremely manual process. As we broadened the use of WITS into other applications for tracking items, we ran across a very unique situation at a very large federal government agency tracking secrets throughout the campus. It was so important to enroll them in the vision of life after WITS.

I was at a National Postal Forum (USPS annual conference with customers) in the 1990s when two gentlemen approached me, displaying official-looking badges, asking if we could go somewhere and speak quietly. They told me they had a high-profile project and that they had vetted me, including a positive reference from senior officials at the USPS. I was then asked to come to their campus, wherein they would divulge the nature of the project. Because I had no security clearance, they said they would continue vetting me. I finally got the invitation to come out.

The project involved the tracking and storage of confidential/secret documents. Their current process involved the use of a multipart form that was signed every time a confidential document was passed from one person to another. Individual parts were then separated and sent to prescribed locations, a very tedious and laborious process for thousands of handoffs. After spending multiple visits researching their needs, a contract was signed for my company to proceed with the project. I then found myself in a meeting room with about fifteen individuals, including procurement, IT and security officers, etc. They expressed how excited they were to get this high-visibility project underway and asked if I could have the system ready for install in two weeks. I said yes.

During the two weeks, I would create their database, including every building, floor, cubicle, desk and storage location as well as every employee's name and associated location. In order to create the database for this project, I asked for their data files containing the information for this matrix. A security officer did not hesitate to tell me they could not provide that to me because it was confidential, and I did not have a security clearance. I stressed that I would not be able to create the database without their files. The response came back: *"Rod, you are a resourceful guy and you will figure that out."* I sat there for a moment then realized I should just shut up, as I was getting some sort of obtuse message. In essence, *I asked myself why I was in the presence of their reluctance and decided not to resist it.*

I packed up my computer, said goodbye and headed

towards the building exit with a security officer escort, as required by protocol. What was a bit strange for me was that the security officer was being quite chatty, not a common trait for someone in his role. As I exited the building, he walked me to my car, also not typical. He then told me how excited they were to get this project going and were looking forward to my return in two weeks. Then, like a scene in the movies, *he placed a floppy disk into my jacket pocket* and said, "See you in two weeks," shook my hand and said goodbye.

I cannot begin to tell you the fear and anxiety that were going through me. *Here I was, standing in the middle of a secured parking lot, with security cameras everywhere, knowing I had confidential data in my jacket pocket.* I left my jacket on, so as not to draw attention, then opened the car door, slid into the driver's seat and placed my hands, ten and two, on the steering wheel, staying far away from my jacket pocket. It wasn't till I got to my airport gate that I found a quiet spot and placed the floppy into my Toshiba laptop (remember orange lettering) and viewed all their data. When I got home, I immediately told Jeri about what had transpired and how concerned I was. For the next few weeks, I continued to be anxious.

The day came for me to fly back, install the software and train them on WITS. It went without a hitch, and during a lunch break, I asked the security officer who had accompanied me to my car to join me alone at lunch. I proceeded to tell him how scared and concerned I had been for the past few weeks. He apologized and reassured me I had nothing to worry about. I then asked for an explanation for the unusual circumstances. He told me how it happened.

Three security officers went into a room with a whiteboard. They placed a message on the top of the board with a question: "How could Rod (expletive) us?" The board was then filled with pros and cons, and after much discussion, they agreed that I was completely trustworthy, and they were dealing with a classic Catch-22 and needed to give me the data. They decided that, while the data was technically confidential, given that WITS automation was a high priority and they couldn't have it without my database design, they decided to release it to me.

What kept me whole through this experience was my vision for their success using WITS. Without my clear vision of what WITS would mean to them, it may not have happened.

RICHARD FINDS HIMSELF

I mentioned that during my days as a Dean of Boys at

Thomas Jefferson how the Love project was so impactful. What was great about the Love Project was that we were able to integrate the approach of contribution into the dean's office. In particular, it gave us options when a student would do something really bad and was subject to suspension or even expulsion. We had this one incident where a very violent student (I'll call him Richard) had a teacher by the throat. He was a student with whom I had carefully developed a relationship where he would call me Rod, so I was able to get control of the situation and brought him to my office. *What's so vivid about his story was how this really troubled boy was able to change his own inner beliefs about himself.*

After speaking with the teacher and finding out what triggered the incident, I presented two choices to Richard, possible expulsion or do something with the Love Project. He reluctantly agreed to take the second. We escorted him to the art department, where we handed him a knife and a block of wood and told him to make something, maybe an animal. He found a picture of a bear, and for three days, he attended no classes and ended up carving a decent replica of a bear.

We then took him to a local hospital, along with his bear carving, and introduced him to a little boy suffering with leukemia. I said to Richard that the boy might enjoy having the bear carving. Richard, without words, handed the carving to the boy, who quietly whispered, *"Thank you."* Richard just stood there in stiff silence; then we left.

In the car, Richard continued his silence until we got back to my office. When I was alone with him, he asked, "What the *expletive* was all that about?" I said, *"Maybe, Richard, that was really the true you who gave that boy the bear. Maybe you are not really this big badass guy who everyone fears but this hurt little boy who no one ever sees."* I then placed my hands on his solar plexus and upper back, a technique I had learned in running the encounter groups to evoke emotion. He then burst into tears, sobbing like a baby as I held him in my arms. It lasted about twenty seconds and he bristled up and said, "You'll never tell anybody about this, will you?" I responded by making him a deal to not say anything if he promised that whenever he felt his violent action coming on, he would seek me out and come to me. He agreed.

About a week later, Richard showed up at my office breathing fire. I closed my door and again touched him to evoke emotion, which worked like a charm, as he again broke down in tears. I knew it was important to keep him close, so I invited him to spend time volun-teering in the dean's office. He did and became a great attribute by calming down other troubled kids when we would pull them into the office because of an incident. At the end of the school year, Richard graduated, to the applause of many, and went on to college. *I was very proud of him because he "chose in" to overcome what was poured into him by life and his earlier influencers. He had truly got beyond some inherited limiting beliefs about himself.*

———

EVERYTHING MUST COME TO AN END

My days at Thomas Jefferson were extremely fulfilling because I could see the effect of my love and commitment to the students. That all changed in 1974, when the gang mentality hit our doors. *In that one year, I was involved in three violent incidents where I was physically attacked.* The last incident involved around seventy-five gang members descending on the school. I attempted to quell their anger, but it only resulted in me being surrounded, knocked down, then brutally assaulted. Fortunately, I'd had the foresight to call the two NYPD officers stationed in our school, before I engaged the kids. The officers arrived within a minute of me being put to the ground and scattered the gang. This was on a Friday and, even though I was quite bruised, I was committed to returning to school on Monday. Over the weekend, my name was in the papers, and my dad, whom I never told how dangerous my job was, read the article. It shook him.

I came back on Monday and went on my usual patrol. I walked into the third-floor boys' bathroom and told the guys to get to class. One of the students, who was physically bigger than me, said, "We're not moving." I asked him why and he said, "You got your ass kicked on Friday." I didn't hesitate, I clenched my fist and slammed it into the books he was holding, knocking them to the ground, followed by my assertively telling him to "get to class". It worked, and the net effect was I again earned their respect.

A month went by and I thought I was in emotional control again; then another incident began to unfold. I was called on to disperse the crowd after being told some of the students had knives. I showed up, but the old Rod didn't. My hands were shaking violently, and it was then I came to the crushing realization that I was in trouble, internally. That incident inspired me to put in for a leave of absence. I was burned out and remembering what I had read in Abraham Maslow's 1943 work on human needs, "A Theory of Human Motivation", I realized "safety" was at the top of the list of my human needs. *I needed a place to go where I felt safe, and I had a place in mind, San Diego, where I would have my second epiphany, this time around money consciousness.*

THE SUIT

I realized one day that my mother had little economic power in our family and that every economic decision, including if I could have the money to buy a new pair of sneakers (athletic shoes to some) to replace the pair I owned with a hole in them, had to be made by my father. My father's response to every request for money was to say *"no"* over and over until, if reasonable, it became a "yes".

Some years ago, before writing this book, I was talking about this very point with my wife, Jeri. She smiled warmly and let me know that throughout our marriage, I too had always said no to almost every request for money by my kids throughout their early life. I have to tell you that this blew me away because I had vowed as a kid that, with my kids, I would be different. In my conscious mind I believed I was operating differently, yet I showed up very similar to my dad. *It was "familiar"*. My thoughtful wife, seeing my pain, softened the blow by pointing out that while it may have been true that I tended to say no at first, when I did turn over, I was more than generous with my response. There I was appreciating the soft landing created by my wife when, out of the blue, a clear memory with my dad came up, helping me to see a significant piece to my *"who I am"* puzzle.

As I mentioned above, my dad had a firm habit of saying no to every request for money. He treated everyone equally, including my mother. So here I am, around eleven years old, being raised Catholic in Brooklyn, NY, and needing a suit for my Confirmation. Being a devout Catholic, my father, in this case, wouldn't dream of saying no to my needing a suit. He took me shopping at Robert Hall, a clothier specialist I had never heard of, and I suspected they would have more expensive clothes than Sears Roebuck, where a lot of my clothes came from.

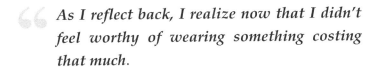

> *As I reflect back, I realize now that I didn't feel worthy of wearing something costing that much.*

When we got there, I found myself feeling very uncomfortable because of the price tags. I had never been exposed to the price of a suit, let alone from a store that, in my mind, was out of our league. *As I reflect back, I realize now that I didn't feel worthy of wearing something costing that much.* Sounds like an inherited limiting thought, doesn't it? I found myself looking for the lowest price tags and, remember, I was eleven at the time.

Suddenly, I noticed my dad was in another aisle, so I walked over, and taking a look at the price tags, I knew he couldn't be thinking about a suit for me at those prices. Well, that day, I discovered a hidden side of my dad I had never seen. He held out a jacket sleeve and asked me to touch it. As I ran my fingers across the cloth, I noticed how smooth it felt in my hand. He looked directly into my eyes and he said, "This is the feel of quality." While I was intrigued, I just assumed he wanted me to at least know what quality was, and I also assumed we would be buying a suit back on the less expensive racks. I couldn't believe my ears when my dad said I should try on the suit I had in my hand.

In disbelief, I carried the suit into the dressing room, full of mixed emotions and confused thoughts. I put it on and, as they say, felt like a million bucks. Then came that voice from within that said the suit costs too much, and I knew my dad didn't like to spend money, and I knew most of all that I didn't "need" a suit of this quality. Wow, was my mind at eleven years old already loaded up with limited thinking chatter.

Well, my dad asked me to come out and model the suit, then asked me what I thought. I wish you could have been in my mind at that moment. First of all, I didn't recall that my father had ever before asked me for my opinion. I was also amazed at the thought that my dad actually saw me as a source of information, which in turn became my first glimpse of my transition into manhood. How appropriate for a Confirmation suit. The other realization I had standing there was that this day was not about my mother, nor about any of my three older sisters, nor about my two older brothers. It was about me.

I stood there like a statue, waiting for the verdict. My father stood motionless and silent for a few moments while I flirted with actually believing he might say yes. Well, too much silence took place, and my mind decided it was time for a reality check. That little voice, deep within, decided enough was enough and proceeded to tell me it cost too much, I would feel out of place wearing it, and my dad really didn't want to spend that kind of money. Boy, was I a busy beaver of negative thought. Suddenly, my thoughts were interrupted when my dad uttered three magic words, "Let's buy it."

I was full of new and uncharted emotions as my dad went to the register, purchased the suit and handed it to me. I remember carrying the suit to the car, feeling like I was carrying gold. My feelings were on fire, feelings I had never known before after seeing a side of my dad I had never seen. He appreciated quality and wanted quality on his son on his special day.

As I think back on that moment, it occurs to me that my dad never said another word about the purchase. We went to the register and then drove home in silence. Unfortunately, later that day this eleven-year-old boy went back to familiar thinking, filling up my mind with thoughts that my father really didn't want to buy it, that he would complain about the cost, and most of all that I really didn't "need" that pricey suit. The bottom line of my consciousness was that I was not equal to the worthiness of that suit. Fortunately, my negative thoughts disappeared on the day of my Confirmation when my dad just smiled at me when I came out of my room in my suit. He was in great spirits and I remember how proud I was on my day of Confirmation wearing that suit. It was like stepping into manhood.

As much as this was a special validating moment in my consciousness, underneath, the core inherited limiting beliefs continued to dominate my essence in many areas, especially in the area of money. I had a lot to work through. Fortunately, as evidenced in my life, I did, and I continue to examine those limited beliefs I secretly inherited.

————

THE PRICE TAG CHALLENGE

I had learned early on, by watching others, that you must look at the price tag before making a decision. When we first met, my wife, Jeri, was amused by my routine when shopping for clothes. I would take my hands, rub the material, and then I would move my hand ever so subtly, and in my mind with no one watching, down to the price tag. Depending on the price, I did all sorts of mental gymnastics. If it appeared high, it was incredibly easy for me to say no, because "that wasn't me". If it was too low, I noticed I would see the clothing was beneath me and meant for someone with less money. Then I would find a price that balanced my thoughts and I would buy the item.

I am blessed to be in a relationship with my "best friend/wife" Jeri, who when she saw how I reacted to price tags, encouraged me to see there was a lesson here, a lesson about overcoming my inherited limited thinking about money and me. One day she asked me to shop with her and asked me to consider approaching the shopping trip to the mall from a different mindset. I said I was game and was curious what she had in mind. *She suggested I consider shopping from a "what do I want" mindset versus shopping from my familiar "what can I afford" mindset.*

Please consider that while some of you may see my rationality as being prudent, also consider that my rationality was a continuation of an inherited limiting thought that I was not worthy of spending that type of money on myself. The other side of this tricky spectrum is blindly spending any amount just to appear "cool" to others.

I began to shop, and my wife kept noticing that I still peeked at the price tags. Being my guide through money consciousness, she challenged me to shop without looking at the price tags. I have to tell you that my mind tried every conceivable way to invalidate this thought; however, my trust in her financial wisdom prevailed and I agreed to go along.

The shopping, or what I now call my spiritual journey through my money consciousness, commenced, and I found myself in men's clothing looking for some shirts that I would "want". It was quite amusing as I found myself struggling to look only at the shirt and not at the price tag and how hardwired my mind was to look, feel, then peek at the price. I finally settled on a shirt I thought I would try on. I was alone in the dressing room trying on this wonderful, rich-looking shirt when the moment of truth came. The self-talk was quite funny. I heard my internal voice actually coaching me that no one would know if I peeked, what's the harm and, in fact, my righteous mind said I had a right to know and I should know to make an informed decision. What a busy mental beaver I was. Well, I'm proud to say I didn't peek and actually had Jeri pay for the shirt and rip off the price tag so I wouldn't know the price.

This was a tough process for me, and I can only

assume that some of you, whether male or female, will read this and will absolutely relate to it. Even if you think you can't relate to this and that Rod Walz is just a guy stuck in his money consciousness, I encourage you to play along and explore the possibility that you may have inherited limiting beliefs about yourself and money, and take what I call "**the price tag challenge**". *(Please note that this is just an exercise and that it is important to be good stewards of our money.)* Just follow the same routine that Jeri had me do the next time you go shopping for yourself (not someone else). It is best if you have a spouse or significant other make the purchase and rip off the price tag. Listen to your self-talk in the dressing room as though you were a paid observer, and most of all enjoy the process of discovering that you have inherited limiting beliefs at some level.

FOURTEEN
FINAL THOUGHTS

I t is so important to embrace the reality that most of your life is no accident. What you attract into your life has everything to do with what you believe about yourself, *in every aspect of your life*. Do you believe and feel that you are worthy and that you have the power to create a life far beyond the life you now have? If yes, then get on with it once and for all. While this is a personal journey, it helps to have others support you. Seek out those who appear to have broken through and get their counsel. Don't waste your time with people who worry about what others think of them. Hang with people who look within for their answers. *Remember, nothing worthwhile happens outside of you.* It is your internal growth that moves you forward.

Beliefs that don't support your vision do not change on their own. It takes diligent focus and an uncompromising *willingness to grow* in order to reprogram your life in alignment with your vision. The more you do it, the easier and more natural it becomes. As I focused on my money consciousness, a key thought that created a huge shift in me was to *bless people with money* and *be in gratitude when paying bills*. Money is meant to flow (responsibly), and when I consistently blessed others with it, it opened up the flow of money through me.

The consistent results in my life bear witness to what can happen when you are willing to examine the beliefs that were poured into you by life and take immediate action towards creating new beliefs when you find that the inherited beliefs are not in alignment with your vision for your life. Focusing on *who you are becoming* really helps your efforts to change.

Look at all sides of your life, do an inventory of where you are in alignment with your vision and where you are out of sync. Be willing to change what is not in sync and take immediate action.

Our life is a journey in which we never fully arrive. Embrace your journey and remember that life puts in front of you exactly what is needed for your growth. Always ask "why am I in the presence of...?" Take a chance and focus on who you are becoming. It can be a miraculous journey if you do so.

Grow well and prosper,
Rod

CONTACT AND MORE INFORMATION

For more information about me and for additional tools to help you.

Website: www.yoursecretinheritance.com
Email: rod@yoursecretinheritance.com

ABOUT THE AUTHOR

Rod is the founder of The WALZ Group and a visionary who, over the past 45 years, has pioneered multiple award-winning enterprise software solutions and services that have significantly improved processes and reduced operational costs of educational, corporate and government entities in the United States.

Beginning in 1976, Rod developed and marketed the first Financial Aid eligibility software in the nation that transformed the approach to analyzing eligibility for loans and grants. In 1981, he introduced the first software program to fully automate the foreclosure process for mortgage trustees in California. During this time, he invented and patented (multiple) the WALZ Certified Mailer™, the first automated form set for preparing USPS® Certified Mail™ that has been marketed nationally to over 3,600 clients with sales of over 300,000,000 WALZ Certified Mailers™. In 1990, he pioneered and marketed the first software application, WALZ Item Tracking System (WITS) used by large corporations and government entities to track "accountable" items such as inbound UPS, FedEx, etc., government secrets, gas cylinders and critical internal documents. In 2002, he developed and introduced the first, highly compliance oriented secure outsourcing service focused specifically on the full life-cycle processing of default and breach notices for mortgage servicers, trustees, foreclosure attorneys and for other consumer debt-related industries accounting for approximately 50% of all residential mortgage delinquencies in the United States.

One of his stated mantras thru life is "to be interested, not interesting", focused on finding needs and creating effective solutions. He retired in 2015 after selling his company.

A native of Brooklyn NY, Rod holds degrees in both marketing and education from St. John's University, including graduate studies at New York University (NYU) and City University in New York. Prior to his entry into the business environment, Rod had an innovative and successful career in the New York City High School system as a Dean of Boys introducing breakthrough programs encouraging students to uncover their true potential.

ABOUT THE AUTHOR

In addition to his contributions at the Walz Group, Rod has spoken at numerous national conventions and, together with Jeri, his wife of 41 years, led seminars on personal growth focused on overcoming limiting beliefs.

185

Made in the USA
Las Vegas, NV
18 February 2022

44157087R00114